LIMITLESS IMPACT

LIMITLESS IMPACT

How Visionary Leaders Build Influence, Scale Success, & Leave a Legacy

©2025 All Rights Reserved. No portion of this book may be reproduced, stored in a retrieval system, or transmitted in any form or by any means—electronic, mechanical, photocopy, recording, scanning, or other—except for brief quotations in critical reviews or articles without the prior permission of the author.

Published by Game Changer Publishing

Paperback ISBN: 978-1-969372-90-2

Hardcover ISBN: 978-1-969372-50-6

Digital ISBN: 978-1-969372-51-3

www.GameChangerPublishing.com

LIMITLESS IMPACT

HOW VISIONARY LEADERS BUILD INFLUENCE, SCALE SUCCESS, & LEAVE A LEGACY

FOREWORD
BY CRIS CAWLEY

Leadership is often measured by milestones such as revenue earned, titles held, or organizations built. Yet true influence extends far beyond quarterly results or personal accomplishments. The leaders who create lasting change are those who look beyond themselves and shape environments where others can grow, contribute, and succeed.

That is the focus of *Limitless Impact: How Visionary Leaders Build Influence, Scale Success & Leave a Legacy.*

This book gathers the perspectives of leaders from a variety of industries and experiences. Each contributor offers insight into what it means to lead with vision, purpose, and responsibility. Although their paths and strategies may differ, they share a common belief that leadership is less about authority and more about service, less about personal gain and more about leaving something meaningful behind as a legacy.

Within these chapters you will find stories of perseverance, lessons shaped through both challenges and achievements, and strategies that continue to prove relevant over time. These stories will inspire you to broaden your definition of success.

Each story reflects a different dimension of what is possible when vision is paired with action.

FOREWORD

The world is calling for leaders who are willing to act with integrity, serve with intention, and pursue bigger goals. This collection is an invitation to step into that role.

May these stories encourage you to pursue leadership that is measured not only by achievements, but by significance. May they remind you that influence is not determined by circumstance, but by vision and choice. And may they inspire you to embrace the truth at the heart of this book that impact is limitless.

CONTENTS

Impacts of the Spectrum *By Ashley Valdes*	1
Lead with Heart, Live With Purpose *By Carolyn Rubin*	19
Teaching With Compassion, Leading With Respect *By Denise Campbell*	33
The Woman Who Chose Herself *By Diana Garcia*	49
K.I.S.S. Codependency Goodbye: Keep It Simple & Scientific *By Eileen Sakofsky*	65
Gracefully Unbreakable *By Emily Kamata*	97
The Catalyst: Life Changing News—Finding Out *By Freideleen (Freddy) Lou*	109
She Rose Anyway *By Kelley Weinzetl*	129
From Crisis to Custodian: The Rise of a Warrior Woman *By Nadia Jacobs*	151
Forged in Fire: Rising from the Ashes of Chaos *By Suzanne M. Saunders-O'Herron, M.Ed*	179

IMPACTS OF THE SPECTRUM
BY ASHLEY VALDES

THE ROOTS OF RESILIENCE

Who am I? As an executive, I report directly to the company president and have a wide range of responsibilities. From worldwide customer relations and retention to training our employees, reviewing contracts, managing operations and logistics, getting involved with the FDA and U.S. Customs, and stepping in to cover for other managers and even the president when he is out of the office—all are duties that fall under my scope of work. Much of my work has transitioned from 100 percent in the office or the warehouse to 95 percent from home.

As a mother, I have two sets of twins who require much attention and affection. My oldest set of twins, now 8 years old, are on the more severe end of the autism spectrum. Often, most of my energy goes to them and their needs. I am their primary caregiver. I homeschool them. I ensure they receive proper therapy. I know their safe foods. I help them with daily living skills. I constantly advocate for more resources and all things in their best interest. Since they are nonverbal, I also have a hidden superpower to understand their wants and needs without words.

My younger twins, now 17 months old, have a whole different set of needs. While they all require constant supervision and my help with daily living—like preparing food, dressing, and toileting—the toddlers need more physical attention. I am always on the move, keeping them from getting into things they shouldn't. Baby-proofing. I also keep an eye out for their developmental milestones and any possible red flags that may affect their development. As a homemaker, I ensure our home is safe, sensory-friendly, and comfortable for us all to grow together.

Where am I coming from? My parents separated and then divorced by the time I was 10 years old. We lost my childhood home in the process. Thereafter, I was constantly moving back and forth between my parents and where they lived; although always left unsaid, it was difficult to feel like I had a stable home. My parents were also seeing other people, and I felt some abandonment during that transition from elementary school through middle school and beyond.

One of the more difficult times was in 8th grade when the grandmother who helped raise me passed away from cancer. At that time, I was already going through a lot; I had been taking part in self-harm, and things came to a serious point of boiling over. I spent a significant portion of my middle and high school years in an emotionally dark place. In addition to these challenges, I consistently struggled with being overweight, a condition that led to bullying. As an adolescent, my peers ridiculed me because of the various diets and programs I underwent to no avail. However, I loved to dance and make music. I would put myself out there on the stage, proudly, regardless.

While I could crack jokes and seem outgoing, it was probably the friends and teachers I had in high school—my lunch crew who would play cards with me, my orchestra family, my theater friends, and my English and art history teachers—that got me through those difficult high school days. Fast forward to my early twenties; I had a knee injury and a lower back injury that required surgery. Post-surgery, I had a hard time letting go of the painkillers, but I made it past that and to the other side. Shortly after, I met the man who would become my husband. Early in our relationship, I had a health scare in which the doctor thought I had lupus, and the treatment for that led to an increased ability for me to become pregnant. We did not know that.

My first pregnancy was scary. I was let go from a new job at the time for missing too many days being sick with all-day nausea. I did not have a stable place to live at the time. I had little support, and I didn't have my own transportation. I relied on government help for medical care. I had only known the father for about eight months, and I had nothing but fear and my gut instincts. The depression was intense. I had to learn to rely on someone I barely knew—who, at that time, hardly spoke to me or even looked at me—who would be the father of my child. Shortly afterwards, we discovered that they were indeed twins. The pressure was on. My first set of twins were premature and had a few health scares of their own, but they, too, are survivors.

Then, at 22 months old, the twins received a diagnosis of autism, leading to the emergence of all the associated questions. About a month later came the absolute biggest scare—I had a revisional stomach surgery that went wrong. The doctors called a code blue and rushed me back into surgery. Before I blacked out, I told the doctor, "Please don't let me die." When I woke up again, I was in the middle of a blood transfusion, freezing, with my husband holding my hand. I think we both realized that moment changed everything in the sense of understanding the true meaning of "in sickness and in health."

These adversities throughout my life taught me the importance of empathy and how to look for the positive instead of focusing on the negative. I understand that every day is a precious gift, and we should cherish each and every day we have. I realized how much inner strength I had, although I didn't see it until I looked back years later. It prepared me to understand better the intricacies of relationships and what was to come. It provided me with an incentive to enhance my work ethic. I was prepared to continue to fight for my family in different ways. Giving up is not an option; resilience is the only way.

Why am I writing this now? I realized that, even within my network, there is a growing number of parents with autistic children. I believe there are many more families facing similar challenges. We all ask ourselves, "What now?" or "Who will understand what we're going through?" I feel a strong calling to build a community where everyone understands each other. So many people feel alone on this journey, and I want them to know that they are NOT alone. We see and appreciate them. It is possible to "do it all" for your family and not lose yourself along the way. I just want to help people accomplish anything they set their minds to for themselves and for their families.

So many others need to know that it is possible to overcome the hardest days. Positively impacting other people's lives—when they want to give up, helping them find their resiliency—is why I am inspired to motivate others through my story.

My readers are likely managing and working their way through a lot of important things all at once: attempting to work or run a business to make a living, managing their homes and their children's schedules with their own, and some may have extra responsibilities of maintaining therapy/doctor appointments, keeping track of and filling out excessive paperwork, and advocating (making phone calls, sending emails, etc.) for their child's needs and resources.

Many of my readers may feel like they are drowning, like they have lost themselves, isolated and unseen. A significant part of my focus is on the harsh realities of navigating through each day with nonverbal individuals, aggressive individuals, and those requiring 24/7 care for daily living, toileting, and hygiene, along with the constant fear or worry about what will happen when we (parents/caregivers) pass away. How will our children, teens, and adults cope? How will they manage their daily living skills, social/emotional behaviors, and other aspects of life with someone who is not us? The scariest question of all is, "Will my child be harmed, abused, or neglected once I am gone?" We may face depression, guilt, anxiety, and other traumatic responses, all while trying to make the best decisions for our children.

Other readers are likely new to the diagnosis of Autism Spectrum Disorder and may have questions about available resources and support. What's next? What should I do? Where can I turn? Circling back, my readers are parents, caregivers, and professionals who are doing their best to balance a chaotic life in a chaotic world. I'm here to tell you that it can be done!

A few major pain points within our chaotic world are a lack of understanding and support, behavioral challenges, financial strain, mental health, and navigating education. Some of my desires, which my readers may agree with, are community and connection, access to information and advocacy, work-life balance, self-care, and resilience.

It has been six and a half years of a nonstop battle since my oldest set of twins was diagnosed with Autism Spectrum Disorder and developmental delays. We are currently conducting new comprehensive diagnostic and psychological evaluations to document the changes that have occurred since those initial diagnoses, and we are finding additional diagnoses going hand-in-hand with autism. I wouldn't say things have become any easier, but every stage over the years has been completely unique. Besides my personal growth mentally and emotionally, my professional growth, having a second set of twins, homeschooling, and everything in between—in addition to doing my fair share (and more) of research, discussion, and learning face-to-face from experts—the undeniable hands-on experiences that life has given me have developed into a specific purpose.

Like other special needs parents, I constantly worry about the future of my children, especially having one child with more aggressive behaviors and both older twins, whom we call "The Bigs," being nonverbal. I have been through, and continue to go through, the hardship of constantly having to fight and advocate to receive support and resources. It's often difficult to get a medical professional or a community resource center to call back promptly. I, too, struggle with my mental health and the weight of what the real life of a mom with autistic children entails.

I hope this chapter will shine a light on the truth behind what caregiving for someone with severe autism while pursuing your own dreams looks like, and that my transformation from a difficult upbringing to a life of purpose will inspire others to keep on fighting. I hope it will show others that while living with special needs children or family members is hard and requires resilience, it is also one of the most impactful lives you can have if you choose to see it that way. I want others to know that they are not alone; they are not invisible, and what they are doing matters!

It's important to understand that, despite very real physical isolation, there exists an extensive group of individuals who share similar experiences. A sense of community and purpose—feeling understood and being able to reach out for anything that is needed (resources, support, venting, etc.)—is so important. I hope you will feel refreshed to know that others share the journey. Together, we continue the conversation on a personal level, provide that sense of connection, and continue necessary advocacy through group activism to create positive changes and limitless impact.

FROM CHAOS TO CALLING: NAVIGATING MOTHERHOOD WITH PURPOSE

Motherhood saved me. I wasn't concerned about being alive before having children. I wasn't concerned about my health; I wasn't concerned about much of anything. When I chose to go down the path of motherhood, it became my responsibility to become responsible. I had to get it together. I had to care. Like the flip of a switch, I improved my work ethic; I improved how I thought about things—my outlook on life changed because I had a more tangible reason to change it. Even more importantly, I finally understood my parents. It helped me to forgive, let go, and grow from what I thought I knew.

As a parent myself, upon hearing of my children's autism diagnosis, I felt all the guilt in the world. All the questions began to run rampant through my mind at all hours of the day and night. Moreover, I didn't initially understand the importance of the resources, support, and community—the importance of complete early intervention. I did not understand that it would be forever. Nor did I know that over the years it would require more and more of me. Since it's a spectrum and you can't truly know the full extent of it at that age (22 months), plus being a first-time mother, how could I have known, and how could I have prepared myself or my children for the severity of autism presenting as profoundly as it is today at 8 years old? Could I handle it? What would the situation mean in the long run? What will other people think? Will they ever be "normal"?

All these questions and unknowns that existed for me exist for every single person who lives with family members who have autism. They are the very questions and unknowns that I constantly receive messages about from other moms, and I work closely with them to try and prepare or support them as best as I can.

In the beginning, I felt like there were a lot of resources for early intervention, and this gave me a sense of false confidence. Over the years, the programs, support, and community seemed to diminish. Everything I once considered important in my life became secondary. The focus entirely shifted to making the best possible decisions for the benefit of The Bigs. As I increasingly shared our story on social media, I realized that there are so many other people going through similar situations and advocating for similar support. I quickly realized that there are various programs for young children with autism through pre-K age and some programs for transitioning adults with autism, but there's a giant gap in resources, opportunities, and certified programs for the everyday child/adolescent with autism in between those ages. My purpose continues to get clearer and clearer as I research and live my own experiences.

So, on top of everything else, I've been furthering my education in social, cultural, and political history because I am convinced that if there aren't enough programs to join or activists focused on autism at local levels, then I need to position myself to create these programs and lead future activists. My belief system tells me that learning about social, cultural, and political trends in the past, plus enhanced personal experiences and stories of others' experiences in the present, can help us all to move confidently into the future with knowledge and a plan of action to create that positive impact.

AUTISM TIMES TWO: THE REALITIES WE DON'T TALK ABOUT

Sometimes you can gauge how the morning will be based on how the night went. On those tougher nights, the sun coming up can bring feelings of anxiety or even dread, because you know that as soon as you hear the first whine from their room, you will not get a moment of peace. My cortisol levels immediately shoot up, and my body is in reaction mode, almost like living with PTSD, and it can stay there for hours, depending on the children's interactions and behaviors throughout the day.

While I know with certainty when my own mental health is in danger—the nonstop vocalizations alone can be enough to drive anyone over the edge—sometimes there is no choice but to push through and start the day. This is where I beg you, if it is even remotely possible, to seek out professional help so that you (and I) are not interacting with our children based on those immediate reactions. Being able to control your own thoughts and behaviors will be huge for the way that your children mimic and deal with their own.

IMPACTS OF THE SPECTRUM

And so begins a routine day: Berberine-infused coffee is my go-to source for energy and for managing my physical pain from PCOS or any possible migraines from losing sleep the previous night. I drink it while preparing a safe-food breakfast for The Bigs and a regular breakfast for The Littles. I make sure everyone (yes, all four of them) gets changed out of their overnight diapers and washed up before eating. Sometimes The Bigs will eat without incident; sometimes they'll refuse or run around or even present a meltdown first; sometimes they'll only want a nutritional shake. My job is to learn to be okay with any option. After eating, we continue the routine of brushing our teeth and getting dressed for the day. The Bigs and I tidy up their room while The Littles stay in their seats or play freely. By 9 a.m. on weekdays, their Registered Behavior Technicians (RBT) arrive, and that is when I breathe my first relieved breath. They are an integral part of our "village" because they know our routine, they know my children, they know me, they help at doctor appointments, they know when it's a good day or a more challenging day, and they treat mine as if they were theirs. They actively participate with the whole family until 3 p.m.

If I didn't prepare the night before, while The Bigs have outside time alongside the RBTs, I gather their homeschool work for the day, set up their tables, and take a moment to start my own work. The Littles have played with every toy in the house by 10 a.m., so it's time for a snack, diaper change, and nap. Around this time is when I get the most work done, answering emails, performing customer relations duties, completing agreements, checking in on warehouse operations, and making myself available to my coworkers via email or phone.

Lunchtime arrives, and I often struggle to introduce new foods to The Bigs, but they always eat something and get supplemented as needed. After lunch, we start homeschooling for the day. We integrate Applied Behavior Analysis (ABA) into their "schooling" just like they would at a regular school, except we allow for much more movement, breaks, less pressure, and more fun! Our goal is to get at least two hours' worth of school time a day, broken down bit by bit, with me "hopping" back and forth between them and my workstation. The Littles wake up around 1 p.m., energized for another round of food, play, and development. Basically, on weekdays, I have learned to spread myself between work, teaching, my own education, and motherhood. Anything is possible! We have a stable routine that allows everyone to get through the day as predictably as possible, and while it can get tedious, others and I can see the improvements in my children and the positive effect that these routines have on all of them. That alone is more than worth it.

There are some days of the week and weekends when my village grows, and I have extra helping hands from my mother or mother-in-law, and extra supervision (or an extra jungle gym in the kids' eyes) from my father. We are fortunate to have them and, despite the difficulties, fortunate that they are willing to be actively involved in our lives. Unfortunately, that is not the case for many families of autistic children. That hands-on support is one of those resources that I look forward to all families having access to in the future.

By the time the evening rolls around, all four children have bathed or showered—The Bigs have been learning to shower almost completely independently, and that is a huge win—and dinner is prepared. All eating times bring about some anxiety in me because while I know the babies will eat anything I cook, their big brothers always pose a challenge. I am grateful every time they eat their food, even if it's another safe food. Now, while there can be some refusals, aggressive behaviors, or meltdowns during the day, the routine helps to keep things at a minimum, which is why that feeling of dread that I mentioned before sometimes comes back when I know the weekend is here.

Weekends are less structured, leading to an increase in challenging behaviors, and I typically find myself alone. The silver lining is that I can focus completely on my kids, playing and responding to them calmly, without the extra workload of my executive day job.

Regardless of the day, The Littles are in bed with "lights-out" by 7:30 p.m. at the latest, and The Bigs are "lights-out" by 9 p.m., sometimes 10 p.m. if we are having a difficult time. While I had trouble accepting the fact that medication was required to get my more aggressive child to fall asleep, research in that area led me to find ingredient-free alternative patches that work for us like a charm. It is all a part of this journey. "Acceptance" is not just something we show every April for Autism Awareness Month, but a skill that we as parents and caregivers practice every single day.

Now, my husband has the kind of alternating manager schedule that is not our favorite thing to work around. Some days he's gone from 6 a.m.

until 6 p.m.; sometimes he starts his shift at 5 p.m. and returns home at 4 a.m. As you might imagine, it is tricky. There are days, however, when their father is off, and yes, I do take advantage to make a little more time to either commute to work and get things done in the office, focus on school, or do anything else that needs to get done outside of the home, including appointments for myself. I also give Dad the opportunity to do what he wants to do with his second day off in the week, and like this, we work as a team to ensure that we are all getting what we need to continue day in and day out.

It is incredibly mentally taxing to carry the weight of all the record-keeping, doctor appointments, constant callings for referrals and evaluations, and therapies, plus the weight of making an income, being a doting wife, the stigma of "stay-at-home mom," keeping things organized and clean, and so on. It is also incredibly lonely and depressing when you have harder days and feel like hope is fleeting. It's difficult to physically get out of the house, it's difficult to maintain friendships and relationships, and it's even difficult to feel like part of the bigger family when you are not invited to gatherings or you know you cannot make it to the gathering for reasons concerning your child. Last, it can become difficult to maintain the connection and spark between you and your significant other, especially when you are overwhelmed, exhausted, and tired of being needed or touched by the end of the day. Time for reconnecting is often difficult to find. It truly is an exhausting and lonely road that people looking in from the outside probably cannot even fathom. It requires the growth of an inner strength that those same people might never have. It's both a blessing and a curse.

More difficult still, my 8-year-olds may never be able to tell me they love me. I may never hear their voices. That breaks me over and over more frequently than I'd like to admit. But I am their voice. I am proud to be their voice for as long as I can to ensure that they receive the best care and live with the best quality of life possible.

I used to think that unconditional love was just a cliché until I loved children with autism who require help, supervision, care, and affection around the clock. I would do anything for them. That's why I keep fighting for them. I keep advocating and being their voice. It often feels like society would rather keep them separated and in the dark, but I refuse to allow that to be their life. They will continue to have experiences like neurotypical children do; they will continue to be included in every aspect of our decisions and family life, and I will keep pushing through the headaches of the extra work and the extra stress because I cannot and will not ever give up on them or the great lives that they deserve. The way I see it, if this has been so taxing on me, I cannot even imagine what it is like in their world, from their perspective.

WEARING ALL THE HATS: EXECUTIVE BY DAY, ADVOCATE BY LIFE

Time management and routine are my absolute keys.

There is a lot of pressure in the realization that if you slack in business leadership or in being a caregiver, then others will suffer from it. While the business aspect of my life could go on without me, the company might suffer from a temporary lack of experienced leadership, and the workload may become too much for others involved. The relationships I've built with our clientele could also suffer. My children, however, cannot live independently without me at this time. Conversely, if you overcommit to leadership or caregiving, the balance will shift once more, resulting in one side losing out. Balance is important, and learning how to maintain that balance is where the real pressure lies.

Another area where I feel fortunate is that I am able to keep open communication with the president of my company about things that go on in my family life, especially if I feel that my work may be affected. In my workplace, we are all able to step up and cover in cases of emergency, and we meet weekly to ensure that the most important tasks are being prioritized—but it is also known that my children's needs are my ultimate priority because they cannot "do" on their own. As life moves so fast and continues to change, I've gained the ability to pivot and apply pressure where it's needed. The "pivot" is another skill that I purposefully pour energy into helping other mothers acquire. For that, I am grateful.

BREAKING DOWN, RISING: MY MOMENTS OF TRUTH

There was one fairly recent moment when I was beyond overwhelmed by everything and everyone. It was one of the lowest lows, if not *the* lowest low, I've felt during my walk in motherhood. I could feel the depression and anxiety. I could feel the tears. I could feel my body so tense, like I was about to be ripped apart. I said out loud to my husband that I didn't want to be their mom anymore. And as soon as it left my lips, I regretted saying it, especially so bluntly. In truth, I didn't mean it. I am exactly where I am meant to be with the children I am meant to raise. But in that one fierce moment, it was not my children that I didn't want to "deal with"; it was autism. I wished that I didn't have to continue living with fighting through the autism every day, because I would never give up my children or put them in harm's way. Again, if it's hard for me, I can't imagine what it's like for them. It's hard to explain because it is part of who they are, and it is inevitable.

That day was one of the hardest days, although there was a silver lining. This was one of those moments when their father realized that I needed help. Shortly after, he confided in me, expressing concern with my appearance, not because I was physically unattractive, but rather because I appeared exhausted and stressed, with swollen eyes and dark circles. I think the experience was his "a-ha" moment, guiding him to include housework and find time in his busy schedule to take over for me so I could have a break. To him, I'd like to say that nothing goes unnoticed and everything is appreciated. Thank you for sticking by my side.

Let's talk about the G-word.

Guilt.

It is easy to feel guilty about the diagnosis itself, placing blame on myself for it being present, although there is no 100 percent clear-cut cause for autism at this time. Then there is the day-to-day guilt of wondering, *Did I react to that properly? Did I do enough for them today?* There's the guilt of wanting things to be different. There's the guilt of wanting other things for myself. The guilt of declining invitations. And the guilt of knowing that one day the responsibilities of being there for "The Bigs" will fall upon their little brothers, "The Littles."

How do I keep going? Aside from wanting the best possible quality of life for my children, I receive a lot of feedback on social media from others who are in similar situations. They let me know that they are watching our journey and that it inspires them. When I look at my children and the people that I am impacting, there's no way I can allow myself to let anyone down.

HOPE AS A HABIT: BUILDING INNER STRENGTH FOR THE LONG HAUL

While I know that not everyone practices this same belief, I believe in God and the power of prayer. There have been many instances where a small amount of faith and the conviction that someone (or something) greater than myself is in charge, by my side, listening to my calls, and catching my tears has enabled me to drift off to sleep at night. As I've said, the path of an autistic parent is often a lonely one filled with questions and doubt, and finding something bigger to believe in, where I don't have to have all the answers, is comforting to me. Shout out to Pastor Furtick for making verses so relatable!

There are days when I need to take myself out of the equation. I need to take a step back and refocus my mind. Being still, quiet in meditation, and sitting with nature, a preference influenced by Ralph Waldo Emerson's "Nature," is a welcome change from the constant noise and physical demands placed upon me while with my children. Last, if—and it is a big *if*—I wake up at least half an hour before my troupe wakes up, I take my coffee and my journal onto the porch and do what I call "3x3 GAGA" journaling. It's something I started completely on my own after reading about the benefits of writing your goals. My 3x3 GAGA breaks down like this:

- List 3 things that you are Grateful for today.
- List 3 Affirmations for the day.
- List 3 Goals, as if you've already accomplished them, for the next three years.
- List 3 Actions you can take today that are in line with your goals.

These practices (prayer, meditation, nature, journaling) give me the space and reinforcement that I need, the "break" that I need, to refocus my mind. These practices allow me to come back to my children or work with a calm demeanor and a clear head. My faith provides me with the spiritual strength to persevere on the challenging path ahead and fulfill my purpose. Through meditation and journaling, I can become grounded and realign my thoughts, my body, and my emotions to carry the weight of my responsibilities without folding. And if I am being completely candid, a good cry can help release any built-up emotional weight. There is no need to be ashamed of that.

Anytime I am feeling burned out or unseen, I do my best to follow the calming practices I've discussed. However, there are days when physical breaks are not workable, and there are no additional personnel available to oversee my team. That is when the bottling up can happen, and the most depression and overwhelm can seep in. In those days, one could feel extra impatient, on edge, or tense. Burnout can easily manifest as physical ailments such as headaches or symptoms similar to the common cold! In 2020, a study was published that revealed that 22.2 percent of the mothers taking part, having children with autism at a median age of 12 years old, who also present aggressive behaviors, show signs of trauma responses mirroring that of PTSD (Post Traumatic Stress Disorder). I find this type of study to be fascinating because I can attest to feeling this kind of response.

When we think about Autism Awareness, we almost always discuss it from the perspective of the diagnosis or those who have been diagnosed. Yet, we rarely discuss Autism Awareness from the perspective of the parents, families, and caregivers who often face the battle with minimal support or recognition. To me, it is pivotal that we look at Autism Spectrum Disorder from all perspectives to provide critical care for the family.

I have a strong belief that once we as a society understand autism from various perspectives, once there is proper training on the subject and how to respond to it within law enforcement and other emergency responders, when medical professionals listen to the concerns of those who spend the most time with the person considered autistic, and once we take into consideration the entirely dismissed mental health aspect of autism and how it affects everyone involved, only then can we truly make a positive impact and become an inclusive society.

Over the years, I have done plenty of exercises to improve my mindset. As I mentioned earlier, I experienced a complete transformation in my life, transitioning from being a negative thinker to frequently finding positive aspects. Like many people, I have read various self-improvement books. I continue to listen to motivational speakers. Even the more cliché practices, like "3x3 GAGA" journaling or looking in the mirror and speaking positive affirmations about myself, my family, my career, our future, increasing income, impact, and so on, are all tools that I have used over the years.

My favorite mantra is one of my own. I always say, "Keep on sparkling!" The dictionary definition of "sparkle" includes "to give off or reflect bright moving points of light," "to perform brilliantly," "to become lively or animated," and my favorite, "to send forth light." When I tell myself or others to "Keep on sparkling," what I am conveying is, keep on shining! Don't let anyone or anything dim your fire! Continue to be a bright light for yourself and others!

A LIMITLESS FUTURE: VISION, IMPACT, AND THE ROAD AHEAD

Just because my plate seems to be full doesn't mean that my dreams are going to stay burning in the oven. There is still a lot of work to do regarding activism and understanding. While I pursue collegiate degrees, I keep my end goal close to my heart. Growing up, fifteen years ago, even five years ago, I would've never fathomed that I would say what I am about to say. My dream is no longer that of a creative yet naïve teen wanting to make music and write songs. Life hit me hard enough to shift my entire trajectory! The impact, while necessary for local communities, is also required far beyond municipal reach. There is a gap between the autism community's needs and government-level support for those needs. The next phase of my life is dedicated to impacting education and legislation for the autism community.

By continuing to share my story and the experiences of my family, I know I can start making an impact right now, right where I am at this moment. And so can you! You and I already have the power to use our voices for change. In the near future, I hope to use this voice through public speaking, podcasts, and writing to continue inspiring others to know that they are so valuable, they are so important, they are doing a wonderful job, and they can keep on sparkling! Not just that they, and you, *can* keep on fighting this great fight, but *how* can we all keep fighting this great fight? While I learn my life lessons, some the hard way, my goals are to turn around and share all that I've learned and continue to learn to benefit the entire community. And yes, eventually, I dream of completing my evolution and going from a naïve teen wanting to write music to a mature mother wanting to write legislation with the needs of our children and the autism community at the forefront.

Impact, visibility, active listening, and community involvement are so important to me because the disconnect that I and many other families know to be true cannot continue. It is plain and simple. These disconnects and gaps in services, resources, support, mental health, and understanding in legislation all have to be addressed with brutal honesty *and* human compassion first in order to pave the way to improved quality of life for families within the autism community and beyond. It is no longer acceptable for parents, caregivers, and those with autism to be treated as invalid. We carry more than the average person can. We do not have to be ashamed. There is not a single good enough reason for us to be shrugged off. We cannot justify the denial of proper care, services, and resources. There is not a single good enough reason for us to continue to accept being unaccepted.

A LETTER TO EVERY WARRIOR MOM

Dearest Wonderful Friend,

I hope this letter finds you in a moment of peace amidst the beautiful chaos that defines your days. I want to take a moment to acknowledge the extraordinary journey you are on as the mother of a child with autism. It's a path filled with unique challenges, profound joys, and a love that knows no bounds.

You may often navigate uncharted waters, facing uncertainties that can feel overwhelming. There are days when you might doubt your strength or question whether you are doing enough. I want to reassure you that you are doing an incredible job. Your love, patience, and dedication are the very foundation upon which your child can grow and flourish, in whatever way that manifests for them. Every small victory, every moment of connection, is a testament to your unwavering commitment.

It's important to remember that you are not alone on this journey. Countless mothers and families are walking a similar path, feeling the same mix of joy and heartache. Together, we create a community rooted in strength and resilience, despite the often overwhelming sense of being alone in the trenches. Reach out, share your experiences, and lean on others who understand the complexity of your journey. If you have trouble finding someone to lean on, then lean on me. There is power in connection, and you deserve that support.

As you face the hurdles that come your way, I encourage you to hold on to this powerful belief: Your love and acceptance are the greatest gifts you can give your child; they will remember your presence most of all. The challenges they face do not define them. Embrace the uniqueness of their mind and spirit. Celebrate every milestone, no matter how small, and remember that progress is not always linear. Your belief in them can light the way, even on the darkest days.

You are not just a caregiver; you are a warrior, a champion, and an advocate. Your love is the most powerful tool you have, and it will carry you both through adversity. Trust in your instincts, be gentle with yourself, and know that you are enough.
With all my heart, I send you strength, hope, and the reminder that you are doing an amazing job. You are not alone, and your journey is valid and worthy of recognition. Keep believing in the beauty of your child and the incredible love you share.

Keep on sparkling!
With warmth and solidarity,
Ashley Valdes

I would love to hear your story; let's connect!

Ashley Valdes is a mother, author, advocate, and homeschooler whose life's purpose is to provide ongoing support to her children and the autism community, to share valuable insights on parenting with multiples, and to foster confidence in homeschooling families. She dreams of making a significant impact on families on a personal level, as well as through legislative efforts by pushing for policies that enhance support and resources for families like hers. She writes books and short stories about her family's journey with two sets of twins—the oldest set having Level 3 ASD/ADHD. She continues in her collegiate endeavors with studies and engagement in the fields of anthropology and sociology, which not only equip her with the knowledge and skills to navigate the complexities of advocacy but also foster personal growth and resilience. Ultimately, her journey is about bridging gaps, maintaining a strong community filled with support and resources, building a more inclusive society for all families, and amplifying the voices of those who often go unheard.

To connect with Ashley:

Instagram: @officialtwinmaker

Community: officialtwinmaker.com

LEAD WITH HEART, LIVE WITH PURPOSE

BY CAROLYN RUBIN

I am Carolyn Rubin, and for more than three decades, I've been a servant leader in healthcare and beyond. But titles never fully captured who I was. I've always seen myself as a healer, a mentor, a bridge-builder—someone who could listen between the lines and see potential before it had a name. I didn't just lead teams. I believed in people. I held space for possibility.

My journey didn't begin with grand ambition. It began with compassion. I started in healthcare because I cared about patients, their families, and their stories. But as I rose through the ranks, I realized that leadership wasn't about climbing. It was about carrying; it was about learning to lift others as I grew.

One of my earliest leadership memories was when a physician pulled me aside after a crazy day. I was a medical assistant, overwhelmed and exhausted, but he looked me in the eyes and said, "You're not just managing patients—you're leading people." That simple sentence awakened something in me. He saw what I hadn't dared to name yet. He gave me permission to own my influence.

That moment lit a fire in me—a calling, not just a career.

I wrote this chapter because I believe women in leadership today need more than strategies. We need a reminder that our impact doesn't have to look like anyone else's to be powerful. We can be strong and soft. Driven and discerning. Strategic and spiritual. We can lead with wholeness—and in doing so, we unlock something limitless.

This chapter is for the woman who has always led from her gut, who feels the weight of others' expectations, and who's ready to rewrite the script. It's for the leader who's navigated burnout and betrayal and is still standing. For the one who's poured into others and wondered if it still matters. Spoiler alert: It does.

As you journey through these next pages, you'll walk with me through stories that shaped my voice and refined my vision. You'll learn what it means to lead with compassion, build cultures of empowerment, see beyond what's spoken, rise from the ashes, and create a legacy that lives now, not later.

By the end of this chapter, my hope is that you'll remember who you are—not just as a leader, but as a soul with something sacred to give. I hope you'll reconnect with your purpose, recommit to your people, and reimagine what impact looks like in your life.

THE HEART OF SERVANT LEADERSHIP: LEADING WITH COMPASSION AND PURPOSE

Servant leadership isn't just a theory to me—it's a calling that has been carved into my character over the course of my life. It's the foundation I return to when I feel off balance, and it's the thread that connects every chapter of my leadership journey. It begins not with command, but with compassion. It's about choosing presence over power and understanding over urgency.

There's a misconception in leadership that showing care somehow compromises authority. I've learned the opposite. When you lead with an open heart, people don't lose respect—they find reason to trust you even more.

I remember a powerful moment that solidified this truth. It was during a time when the organization I was working with was experiencing rapid change—new policies, budget cuts, shifting leadership. I was in back-to-back meetings, pulled in a dozen directions. One afternoon, a team member passed me in the hallway. She had always been kind and respectful, never one to ask for anything. But this time, she stopped and looked like she was about to speak, then hesitated. I paused and asked, "How can I help you?"

She looked down, clearly unsure whether she could share. I waited gently. Finally, she said, "I've worked here for 18 years, and I've never been asked what I think. I just... I think there's a better way we could check patients in so rooms are turned around faster. It's been frustrating because no one seems to notice."

I stood there stunned. Her idea was simple but brilliant. It would save time, improve efficiency, and support patient satisfaction. But what struck me most wasn't the suggestion—it was the fact that it had taken nearly two decades for someone to invite her voice. That moment shifted me.

I gathered my team the next week and began what would become a monthly "Listening" session, where we invited input from staff at every level. Not only did innovation soar, but morale did too. People felt seen, and when they feel seen, they show up differently.

That's the power of servant leadership. It reminds people they matter.

And yet, this kind of leadership requires discipline. It asks us to slow down when everything around us is speeding up. It demands that we choose curiosity over assumption, dignity over directives. It's not the easiest path—but it's the most impactful.

Another story comes to mind. I was mentoring a team leader who was struggling to manage a high-performing yet emotionally volatile employee. "I just don't know how to deal with him," she admitted. "He gets defensive no matter how I give feedback."

I asked her, "What do you know about his story?" She blinked. "His... story?"

"Yes," I said. "Not his résumé—his story. What shaped him? What motivates him? What might he be protecting when he gets defensive?"

A week later, she returned changed. She had taken the time to ask him about his life—about the challenges he'd faced, his upbringing, the things that mattered to him. She said, "I didn't fix him. But I understand him now. And that changes how I lead him."

Leadership isn't telling people what to do. It's reminding them who they are. It's saying: You belong. You matter. And I see you. So when you walk into your next meeting, your next coaching session, your next hallway conversation—don't just ask, "What needs to be done?" Ask, "Who needs to be seen?" That's where impact begins.

FROM ADVOCATE TO ARCHITECT: BUILDING CULTURES OF EMPOWERMENT

For much of my early leadership, I saw myself as a defender. I stood in front of my teams like a shield—advocating for what they needed, pushing back against poor decisions, protecting them from toxic environments. I was proud to be the one who "had their back." And to be honest, it often earned me trust.

But over time, I began to notice a pattern. Every fire that started, I ran to put it out. Every policy that felt unfair, I stood up to challenge. Every broken system, I patched. The problem? I was busy being the fire extinguisher, but I wasn't designing anything to prevent the sparks.

That realization hit me like a brick. I was exhausted. And worse, I was unintentionally reinforcing dependency. People knew I would fight for them—but I hadn't always equipped them to fight for themselves.

That's when I began to shift from advocate to architect.

I started seeing leadership not just as a role to protect, but a space to design. Leadership is architecture. You don't just respond to what is—you create what could be. You cast vision, lay foundation, build systems, and empower the people who live within them.

I once inherited a team known for "high turnover and low trust." When I stepped into the role, I was warned, "Don't expect too much from them." But I didn't see brokenness—I saw untapped brilliance. And I didn't just want to advocate for them—I wanted to build with them.

The first step? Listening.

We held design sessions, not just meetings. I asked questions like:

- "What would make this a place you're proud to work?"
- "What would it take for you to feel empowered?"
- "What does leadership mean to you?"

The answers became our blueprint.

Together, we built new communication protocols, revised outdated workflows, and created peer mentorship teams. More importantly, we created ownership. People weren't waiting for me to fix things anymore—they were finding solutions themselves.

We implemented what I called the "Foundation First Framework":

Vision Clarity – What are we building, and why does it matter?
Shared Values – What do we stand for, and how do we show up for each other?
Empowered Structures – What systems help us grow without gate-keeping?
Feedback Loops – How do we assess, adjust, and evolve—together?

Within a year, turnover dropped by 45 percent, and internal promotions rose dramatically. But the most meaningful change? People began saying, "I feel seen here. I feel safe here. I feel strong here."

As leaders, we often think we need to be the hero. But real leadership is about removing yourself as the bottleneck. It's about building systems that thrive whether you're in the room or not.

There's a big difference between advocating for people and empowering them.

Advocacy says, "Let me fight this battle for you."

Empowerment says, "Let me equip you to lead in any battle."

Both are important. But only one is scalable. Only one creates cultures where people stop waiting for permission—and start leading with purpose.

I saw this firsthand when one of our junior team members noticed a process gap that affected patient flow. In the past, she might've kept it to herself or expected leadership to solve it. But this time, she took initiative, created a draft solution, and presented it in our innovation huddle. The solution? Simple. Impactful. Implemented within a week.

That's what happens when people feel they have ownership.

As a leader-architect, your job isn't to design every detail. It's to create the structure where others can design within it. It's to make space, set standards, and then let go. It took me years to understand this, but once I did, it changed everything:

If you want to build a culture that lasts, you can't just put out fires. You must build fireproof environments.
Ask yourself:

- Am I spending more time reacting or designing?
- Do people come to me only for answers, or do they feel empowered to lead?
- Am I building something that can thrive without me?

Being an advocate made me feel needed.
Being an architect made me feel useful.
And that distinction is what allowed me to multiply my impact, not just protect it.

LISTENING WITH YOUR EYES: SEEING BEYOND WORDS

Leadership isn't just about what you hear—it's about what you sense. It's reading the room when the words say one thing, but the energy says something else. It's noticing the slump in someone's shoulders, the hesitation in their voice, the brilliance that flickers just beneath the surface of silence.

This is what I call "listening with your eyes." It's an essential leadership skill, especially in environments where people have learned to stay silent to survive. If you wait for people to speak their truth, you may wait forever. But if you learn to "see" them, you'll begin to hear what they've been longing to say.

One afternoon, I was facilitating a team meeting about upcoming changes to our operating procedures. I noticed one woman—let's call her Dana—leaning back in her chair, arms crossed. She wasn't being disruptive, but she wasn't engaged either. While others nodded along, Dana remained still, silent, and slightly withdrawn.

After the meeting, I asked if she'd stay behind for a moment. I didn't accuse. I didn't confront. I simply said, "I noticed something felt off for you in the room. You okay?"

She exhaled and dropped her shoulders. "I've seen so many changes that were just for show. It's hard to believe this one will be any different."

There it was—not resistance, but resignation. She wasn't a problem employee. She was a leader waiting to believe again. But until someone paused to see her, she had no reason to speak.

That moment reminded me of something I deeply believe:

People aren't hard to reach—they're tired of not being heard.

In high-pressure work cultures, especially in healthcare and corporate settings, people often wear professional masks. They show up, perform, comply—but they don't reveal their full truth. And if we, as leaders, don't slow down long enough to notice, we miss the deeper stories unfolding in every room.

I started building intentional practices into my leadership to stay attuned. Here's one I call the 3-Second Presence Rule:

Before you respond, pause for three seconds.

One second to breathe.

One second to make eye contact.

One second to choose intention over reaction.

It's a small shift with a massive impact. It allows you to stay grounded and attuned. In those three seconds, I've noticed nervous glances, clenched fists, and unshed tears. I've also seen subtle sparks—when someone is excited but unsure if they have permission to speak.

That's another crucial part of listening with your eyes: recognizing potential before it's vocalized.

One of my most talented team leaders today was once a painfully quiet intern. In our early meetings, she rarely contributed. But I noticed she took copious notes and had a calm, observant presence. After a few weeks, I asked her directly, "What are you seeing that we might be missing?"

She blinked in surprise and cautiously shared a few insights. They were sharp, nuanced, and incredibly helpful.

I said, "I want you to speak up more. What you see matters."

Later, she told me that moment changed her entire view of leadership. "You didn't wait for me to speak up—you invited it. And that made me believe I had something worth saying."

That's the difference presence makes. You become the mirror that reflects someone's worth back to them before they're ready to name it themselves.

In today's fast-paced world, where everything is scheduled down to the minute, emotional intelligence often takes a backseat; it's not optional—it's foundational.

We don't just listen for updates. We listen for understanding. We don't just manage tasks. We tend to people. We listen for the sighs between the words, the excitement behind the hesitation, the courage behind the confusion.

Here are a few tools to help you listen with your eyes:

Silent check-ins: At the start of meetings, observe before speaking. What's the body language saying? Who's present but disengaged? Who's eager but holding back?

One-on-one walk-and-talks: Movement opens up conversation. People are often more honest in motion than in meetings.

Reflective listening: Mirror back what you observe. "I noticed you got quiet when that topic came up. What was going through your mind?"

Remember: Most people don't need you to fix their problem. They need you to see them in it. When someone feels seen, they feel safe. And safety is the foundation of all true transformation.

So the next time you step into a room, don't just bring your agenda. Bring your attention. Bring your curiosity. Bring your presence.

That's how you listen with your eyes. That's how you build trust before a single word is spoken.

TESTED BY FIRE: RESILIENCE AND RENEWAL IN LEADERSHIP

There's a side of leadership that doesn't make it into the conference keynotes or glossy LinkedIn posts. It's the side where your heart breaks, your confidence shatters, and your convictions are tested in ways you never anticipated. It's the part where leadership stops being theory and becomes a furnace.

I've walked through that fire more than once.

There was a season in my leadership when everything I had built felt like it was crumbling. I had been betrayed by someone I mentored closely —someone I had poured into, coached, and championed. Their actions not only blindsided me, but they also caused deep division within my team. The fallout was both personal and professional.

At the same time, I was pushing myself beyond healthy limits. I believed I had to be the strong one. The glue. The problem-solver. I couldn't show weakness—at least that's what I told myself.

But the truth was, I was unraveling.

I began waking up in the middle of the night, heart pounding, mind racing. I felt isolated and disillusioned. I questioned my instincts. I questioned my worth. I even questioned whether I wanted to lead at all anymore.

One afternoon, I found myself sitting in my car in the parking lot, unable to walk inside. I gripped the steering wheel and whispered, "God, if I'm going to keep doing this, I need a different way. I need you in this."

That moment was my breaking—and my breakthrough.

It was there, in the stillness of exhaustion, that I heard what I hadn't made space for:

Leadership doesn't require perfection. It requires your presence.

That moment marked the beginning of my renewal.

I stepped back—not out of the calling, but into a recalibration. I leaned into my faith, my family, and my own healing. I sought out a coach and a counselor. I redefined success—not as how much I could carry, but how well I could align with what mattered most.

What I discovered is something every seasoned leader eventually faces:

You will be tested—not to break you, but to burn off everything that isn't aligned with your true calling.

The fire strips away performance. It refines identity. And in its aftermath, you don't just return stronger—you return authentic.

One of the hardest yet most important lessons I learned was this:

Resilience is not endurance. Resilience is renewal.

Endurance can make you numb. But renewal brings you back to life.

That meant giving myself permission to rest. To grieve. To let go of roles, relationships, and rhythms that no longer served the leader I was becoming. It meant no longer leading from scarcity or fear of being replaced—but from trust in who I was and who I was meant to empower.

As I reentered leadership with a new lens, something shifted.

I no longer sought to prove myself—I chose to be myself. I no longer needed to have all the answers—I was comfortable asking better questions. And I no longer saw setbacks as failures—I saw them as formation.

Over time, the relationships that had been fractured began to heal.

New partnerships emerged. And most importantly, my leadership deepened—not because I was tougher, but because I was more transparent.

I began sharing my story with others—first quietly, then more boldly. What surprised me most was how many leaders came forward with their own stories of burnout, betrayal, and breakdowns they never dared to voice. We had all walked through fire. But until someone spoke it aloud, we thought we were alone.

That's why this chapter matters. That's why your story matters.

You are not weak because you've been wounded. You're wise because you've walked through it.

And if you're in the fire now—whether it's internal struggle or external chaos—know this: The fire will not destroy you. It will define you if you let it.

Let it burn off the people-pleasing.

Let it burn off the perfectionism.

Let it burn off the pressure to carry everything alone.

What will remain is gold.

So if leadership feels heavy right now… pause. Breathe. Go inward. Let yourself heal. You don't have to rise instantly. But know that when you do, you'll rise deeper. You'll rise clearer. You'll rise whole.

And that version of you? She's unstoppable.

LEGACY IN ACTION: EMPOWERING THE NEXT GENERATION

Legacy is a word that often gets reserved for the end—something we reflect on after retirement, or something written in a eulogy. But I've come to understand legacy differently.

Legacy isn't what you leave after you're gone.

Legacy is what you build while you're here.

And the most powerful legacies are not built in boardrooms—they're built in moments. Quiet ones. Consistent ones. Intentional ones.

Years ago, I met a young woman named Angie. She was new to the organization, full of potential, but unsure of her voice. I saw myself in her —the quiet strength, the hunger to learn, the fear of getting it wrong. She was technically skilled but hesitant to lead.

One day after a team presentation, I pulled her aside. "You asked a question today that shifted the entire conversation," I told her. "Do you know how rare that is? You see things most people overlook."

Her eyes welled with tears. "I've always felt that. I just didn't know anyone else saw it."

That moment sparked something in her. From that day on, I invited her into higher-level meetings, asked her opinion in public forums, and gave her stretch assignments that challenged her to grow. She didn't always feel ready, but she always showed up. And over time, she began mentoring others, stepping into more influence, and crafting a leadership style that was both bold and deeply authentic.

Years later, she became a director. She thanked many people, but then she looked at me and said, "You didn't just lead me. You believed in me when I wasn't sure I belonged in the room. You made space before I earned it. And that space changed everything."

That's legacy.

Not your accolades.

Not your salary.

Not your title.

Legacy is the person you mentored who's now mentoring others.

Legacy is the system you changed that still empowers people long after you're gone.

Legacy is the belief you planted in someone that now bears fruit in places you'll never even see.

Leaders understand that leadership is not accumulation. It's multiplication.

We don't hoard wisdom—we share it.

We don't gatekeep opportunities—we open doors.

We don't cling to our seats at the table—we build longer tables.

This kind of legacy demands intentionality. It means looking for the next generation, not waiting for them to prove themselves. It means creating opportunities, not just offering advice. It means choosing to lead in a way that makes others feel more powerful, not more dependent on you.

One of the ways I've committed to living legacy in real time is by creating mentorship rituals—monthly one-on-ones with rising leaders, "feedback forward" circles where everyone gives and receives growth input, and reverse mentoring sessions where I learn from younger professionals with fresh perspectives.

But it also shows up in the smallest moments.

The email of encouragement sent after a tough presentation.

The invitation to lead a project even when someone's only 80 percent "ready."

The way you model boundaries so others feel permission to protect their own peace.

Every interaction is a seed. You never know which one will take root.

A dear colleague once said to me, "You leave fingerprints on people that they carry into rooms you'll never enter."

That stuck with me. Because that's exactly what we do as leaders.

You may never know the full extent of your impact. But that doesn't mean it's not unfolding every single day.

Here's what I know for sure:

Someone is watching how you handle conflict—and learning grace.

Someone is watching how you bounce back from setbacks—and learning resilience.

Someone is watching how you empower others—and learning humility.

Your leadership story isn't just yours. It's becoming a map for someone else.

And you get to decide what kind of path you're drawing.

So as you think about your own legacy, don't ask, "What will I be remembered for?"

Ask, "Who am I building while I lead?"

Because at the end of the day, your impact isn't measured by the size of your platform.

It's measured by the lives you touched.

And by the leaders who rise because you chose to lift.

Your impact isn't in the spotlight.

It's in the ripple.

And that ripple? It's limitless.

If you take one thing from this chapter, let it be this:

Your presence is your power.

You don't have to become someone else to lead well. The world doesn't need more perfection—it needs more truth. More heart. More courage. More you.

To the women who've walked this journey with me to the end: Thank you. Your leadership matters. Your story matters. And you matter—deeply.

If this chapter spoke to your soul, I invite you to continue the conversation. Let's connect. Whether you're ready to mentor others, lead with intention, or simply remember who you are, I'm here to walk with you.

Because your impact? It's limitless.

Carolyn Rubin is a nationally recognized transformational leader, empowerment coach, and award-winning healthcare executive with over 32 years of experience in patient advocacy, team development, and heart-centered leadership. Known for her unwavering commitment to servant leadership, Carolyn has spent her career elevating others, whether through mentoring emerging leaders, advocating for patient-centered care, or creating programs that foster personal and professional reinvention.

Her coaching approach blends strategy with soul, helping women and teams lead with emotional intelligence, resilience, and purpose. As the founder of EmpowerFuse™, Carolyn amplifies the voices of women and professionals ready to unlock their inner power and lead with authenticity. She also hosts and contributes to platforms that inspire faith-based transformation and personal breakthroughs, drawing from her own lived experience of rising through adversity with grace.

Carolyn's impact extends far beyond corporate corridors—she has helped countless individuals align their passion with their profession, rewrite limiting beliefs, and embody the courage to lead boldly. Her message is simple yet powerful: *You don't need to be saved. You just need to be shown how to unlock the power within.*

Carolyn continues to inspire a movement—one that empowers the next generation to lead from the heart and leave a legacy of compassion, courage, and conviction.

LEAD WITH HEART, LIVE WITH PURPOSE

To connect with Carolyn:
—

LinkedIn: http://linkedin.com/in/carolynrubin
—

Website: www.carolynmrubinconsulting.com
—

Website: https://www.carolynmrubin.com
—

Empowerfuse: https://m.youtube.com/@empowerfuse

TEACHING WITH COMPASSION, LEADING WITH RESPECT

BY DENISE CAMPBELL

I have been working in education in a variety of sectors for over 34 years. Education has always been a part of my being. My mom was in education, and although I investigated other careers, it was like Kermit the Frog's "Rainbow Connection":

> *Have you ever been half asleep*
> *and heard voices?*
> *I've heard them calling my name.*

No matter what other careers I thought I might pursue, education always called me back. When I finished my degree and got my certification, I was living in a small Missouri community of about 70,000 people. I started my career by teaching at a behavioral preschool while also teaching at a juvenile detention center and working with adults with mental illness. The extremely varied experiences I had during my first year of teaching helped to form my values as an educator.

I moved into general education in an elementary school setting the following year. My time teaching there started my journey as a classroom teacher. After moving to Fort Worth, I taught in a school that was considered to be in Crip gang territory.

I taught sixth grade for many years there. During that time, the administrative team told me that they felt that I would be a great candidate for the administrative cohort college program. I was soon on my way to begin my career in administration and to be an instructional leader to students and teachers.

I began as an assistant principal at a middle school and later at a high school. After five years as an assistant principal, I transitioned into a principal role. I was a principal for twelve years total, five years in Missouri and seven years in Phoenix. My schools were preschool through eighth grade. I loved the time being able to teach kids as well as influence and work with teachers. After my years as a principal, I moved into a position as director of curriculum and instruction.

I realized after about a year in that position that although I was working with principals, I missed the time I had spent working with students. I went back to teaching. I've spent the last sector of my career teaching special education within the general education setting.

During my time teaching, I was fortunate to be the mother of three wonderful children and four awesome grandchildren. While my kids were school-aged, I tried to be available and focused on their activities and their lives and not put my job first. Family first, job second.

I tried to instill this in my teaching staff when I was a principal as well. I didn't want to be that educator mom whose kids talked about how their mom wasn't around for them. I developed strategies that could be used in the classroom to help students feel important without taking valuable time away from my family.

I am writing this with the hopes that I can encourage and motivate educators to see how they can be an influence on students and other educators without spending their valuable personal time. Work/life balance is important, and spending time during the school day to help kids feel seen and valued can help teachers protect their time away from school as well as build a much-needed positive culture in the classroom and school.

VALUE AND RESPECT

When I was a sixth-grade teacher, I used something that I called "gotchas." They were little slips of paper that I would give to students who were working hard, being nice to others, standing in line quietly—all those different things that we want kids to do within the classroom. I would hand them out at the beginning of the year like popcorn, or like Oprah, "You get a gotcha, and you get a gotcha," just to let kids know that they were doing great things. Most of the time, I would not tell them why; I just set it on their desk. They put their name on it, and it went into a bucket on my desk. Every Friday, I drew approximately five slips from the bucket, and as each name was called out, they got to choose one wrapped item. I would wrap random things that I knew they really liked, anything from flavored lip gloss or smelly lotion to a baseball or football card, hair clips, and so on. The items would reflect their interests. I would specifically get things that I knew they liked because it was something they wore, talked about in class or recess, or asked for at times. This helped them to feel seen and heard. They would get to unwrap it and see what they got after all the names were drawn, and if they wanted to exchange with others, they could. Then we dumped the gotchas and started over the following week. The nice thing about the gotchas is that they were not used as "classroom currency." They didn't have to save them up to "purchase" items at various gotcha prices or turn them in to purchase a missing pencil or pay because they were missing their name on a paper. Yes, I have seen those things happen in a classroom. I have seen teachers try to use tickets or slips, where they would give them to the kids as a reward for great things they were doing, but they used them as a kind of token currency. If they forgot a pencil, they would say, "Oh, you have to give me five tickets to get a new pencil." That takes away from the goal of kids feeling valued for doing great things.

The students would simply put their name on it and put it in a bucket. Everyone had the chance to get a prize. I know, there are always "those kids" who don't have as many gotchas in the buckets as others, and the chances that they would get a prize were slim. There were times when I specifically had prizes that my toughest student would really want, and yes, I palmed their name, swirled the tickets in the bucket, and boom, magically pulled their name. Why? It gave that student a chance to be noticed and for their good behavior or good deeds... to be valued. Often, the other students would get excited for the student as well. I would always try to say something like, "Wow, it was a great week for you!" Slowly, the attitude and behavior of that student would change. We want to ensure that when we give rewards to students, it's not a token system; they are receiving that reward because they are valued. They're valued as a person. They're valued as humans. They're valued as kids who are learning to do great things in their lives. As teachers, we are there to foster and motivate their learning, whether it is socio-emotional or academic. This was just one of many fun exchanges I would have with the students during the day, week, and year.

Building value and positive relationships with the students was very important. I'm not saying I am there to be a student's friend, but I am there to be positive and friendly. Sometimes, school is the best place students have in their lives. I show students I value them first before I expect them to value me. I have done this both in the classroom and as a principal. I do this by simple conversations with kids or classes to help students feel seen and heard. I write important things students tell me in my planner so that I can remember to check back with them about things they tell me. Anything from a big game coming up, a performance of some kind they'll be in, a feeling of anxiety or sadness over a specific event, just to name a few. As an educator, I am so busy with my professional life and personal life that it is easy to forget things that students tell me. I find that when I put a "check back" note in my planner, it really helps the student feel I listen to them and value what they tell me. If I had a student who was going to be in a play or a student who had a big football game coming up, I would write it in my teacher planner so that on that day I could say, "Good luck with your game," or "Break a leg on your performance." It really helps kids to feel valued and heard. Their faces often light up when I ask them how an event was or ask them how they are feeling. Because I took the time to remember what was going on in their lives, it helps them know that they have value in their lives. That's one of the most important things when building a classroom culture or a school culture: kids and families feeling valued. Allowing children to express their feelings, whether joyful, sad, or worrisome, shows that they are valued as individuals and their feelings are valid, too.

When I work with kids who have had behavior issues, I always say something like, "I don't like what you did when..." or "You really hurt that person's feelings by..." and then I follow up with "What is going on?" The simple "What is going on?" has opened up a plethora of conversations. It's important that we get to know our students so that we can begin to understand the *why* of the way they are acting. I find that knowing the why isn't just important for the struggling student, but also for the thriving student. When I know what drives that student or their strengths, I can build on those strengths. Even if it is that they are the "expert for the day" and can go around and help others.

When I walk through the hallway, I always say hello to the kids or wave if they are in a silent line. Even students I don't know well. I try to be in the hall at the end of the day just to say, "Hi, how's your day?" or "Have a fantastic afternoon!" I want kids to leave the school feeling that they are important and valued. When somebody is looking sad, I try to ask, "Hey, are you having a bad day? What can we do to make it better?" Treating kids with the dignity and respect that we want to be treated with helps them feel better, feel important, and feel seen and wanted. There have been times when I needed to refer the student to our counselor or social worker. If I had walked by without showing the student their feelings were just and they were valued, they would have continued to feel sad, unvalued, and unseen. I always think about how I would want someone to treat my kids. What are those aspects that you want?

Because I am a general education/special education teacher, I have the opportunity to walk into a variety of classes or to often see teachers with kids in the hallway. One of my favorite things to say is, "Oh my gosh, you've got some of my favorite kids in here." Those kids never know who my favorite is, but it helps them feel good. I had kids say, "Oh, am I your favorite?" I only respond, "Oh, if you think you're my favorite, you must be my favorite." It's a fun and simple way for kids to feel seen and valued.

Showing students that they are valued by the teacher—and teaching and modeling value in the classroom—fosters a classroom of respect. Respect is a two-way street, but I always show the students respect and value first and foremost. Respect and value become a reciprocal model when children feel valued and respected and are taught to respect others. They will respect and value you as a teacher or an educator. Children will more often remember how you made them feel than any curriculum you taught. If you ask anyone what they remember from school, they will always talk about a teacher who made them feel good and valued as an individual.

RESPECT AND COMPASSION

One year, I decided that I would create postcards for each of my students. I addressed the postcards and placed a stamp on them so they were ready to go. Once a week, I would pull one postcard out of a box. I would sit down and think about one, maybe two great things that I could say about the student whose postcard I had pulled. I wrote the wonderful things that I observed about their child. It could be anything like, "I am so excited to tell you that I saw Bob helping someone on the playground. The student fell, and he ran over to help her up. What a wonderful act of kindness!" Or, "I am so excited that while we were reading aloud, Bertha usually doesn't want to read, but she raised her hand and took the chance to read aloud and did such a great job. What a huge accomplishment!" I would sign them and send them off in the mail. Students would tell me that the postcards were on the refrigerator for everyone to see because their parents were so proud of the note. One student told me her parents wouldn't take it down. I jokingly said I would send a larger one next time.

One year, I noticed that many of my postcards were being returned due to the wrong address or because the student had moved. This had become one of my favorite things to do. So I thought, *Okay, I'm going to have to do this differently.* I put student names, parent/guardian names, and phone numbers on the cards. I decided that I would start making phone calls. I was teaching sixth grade in a middle school setting. This was not going to be as quick and easy as the postcards. I designated a specific day for the various periods (i.e., Monday 1st period, Tuesday 2nd period, and so on). That way, I could make a phone call during my planning period and still have time to do the rest of my teacher-related duties. I would call to inform the adult living with the student about the great things their child had done or what was wonderful about their performance. This was just what I did with the postcards. I always started the phone call with, "Hey, this is Ms. Campbell. I am calling about Bob; he's not in trouble..." And then I would start saying what great things their child was doing. I usually got a "Thank you for calling," or they said they appreciated the phone call. I had one parent who just started to cry on the phone and said, "I have never had any teacher call or tell me anything nice about my child." I really had to hold back the tears. It sucks that a parent has never received a phone call with something good about their child. In the six years of parent/teacher conferences, they never heard anything positive about their child. The empathy I had for that parent influenced me to continue to send postcards and make positive phone calls. Compassion for students and parents goes a long way. Families send the best students they have to school every day. The students in our classrooms are their pride and joy. As an educator, I constantly challenge other educators to have the compassion to find the good in every student. The compassion I showed to the families by telling them "something good" about their students spilled over to respect for me as a teacher. Because I had the compassion to find and say something nice, it opened the door for respect if I ever needed to make that dreaded call or have that dreaded parent-teacher conference. When I was principal, I challenged my school to do this. The postcards helped foster a change in the culture of the school to be more compassionate, empathetic, and kind towards others. Note, I said it *helped* to change the culture of the school. Fostering compassion in the classroom is much easier than within a school. I don't just send home the notes or make the phone calls; I also take the time to tell the kids great things to their faces.

If students have been absent, I tell them they were missed. If they are late to school, I tell them I'm so glad they're at school. Kids feel comfortable and confident in my class because I speak to them with respect, with encouragement, and in a friendly tone. That is what I expect of my students as well. Don't get me wrong, there are times I raise my voice, but I always follow it up with "Oh my gosh, I had to use my mean teacher voice! I'm so sorry. Give me a moment to find my nice teacher's voice." I take some deep breaths and refocus and say, "Okay, now that I have my nice teacher's voice back, let's..." A great teaching moment on how to refocus for the moment.

As educators, we're here to teach kindness, respect, and compassion. We need to build a sense of compassion in our classrooms. A big buzzword that we use now is "social emotional learning." Within that, we teach compassion, but teachers have been teaching/fostering compassion for the 34 years I've been teaching. The compassion that we teach students is so very important. Not all students know how to be compassionate because they either don't experience it at home or don't have opportunities to demonstrate it at home. I always take time in the day to have kids talk to each other cordially, and I lead that conversation so that if somebody says something that is unkind, I can step in and say, "Oh, how could you say that differently? That was kind of hurtful." I also help foster the conversation if the kids get to a point where they just don't know what to say.

I give the kids respect and speak to them with kindness and compassion from day one as a teacher or as an administrator. As educators, we must help foster positive and caring relationships with kids. As I foster the students' understanding of how to be kind and understand each other's feelings, the classroom dynamics change. As an administrator, I saw a classroom where my thought was, *Does this teacher really like kids?* My heart goes out to the kids who feel disliked by their teacher. The teacher was not respectful to the kids, and the kids were not respectful to each other. The teacher spoke disrespectfully to the kids more often than she was compassionate or kind. The teacher would sit in a chair and *teach* a lesson, and then say, "Go sit down and do it." If the kid said, "I need help," the response was, "I already taught it to you. You should know it." She did not work with the kids, she did not take an interest in the kids, and she did not speak to them with respect and kindness. When the students asked what she did for Thanksgiving, she said, "None of your business." Yikes! Guess what happened? The kids weren't respectful and compassionate toward her either. The dynamics of that classroom started to change. As the year went on, the kids started becoming less respectful, less kind, and less compassionate toward each other. They were great kids the year before. They were great kids at home, but when they were in that classroom setting, the culture of that classroom was hateful; it was not compassionate or respectful. This is an example of how one teacher can make a difference, positive or negative. It starts with the teacher, the educator, the principal. As a principal, I helped set the culture in the school. As an educational leader, I worked with teachers to develop their craft and help and encourage them to create a positive culture in their class.

I worked with this teacher and taught her to give kids respect and compassion. To treat the kids as she would want to be treated. One of the ways I worked with her was to give kids compassion for not knowing something and to show respect and compassion during the learning process. If a student says, "I don't understand this," respond with, "Is there anyone else who does not understand that? Let's come back to this table. Let's come to the carpet and talk about it." I modeled learning and teaching expectations. I had a group that I was working with. I taught the lesson, and then I said, "If you think you know it, you go back to your seats and start working on this math lesson. If you're still unsure about it, stay here on the carpet with me. We will work on this together. If you go back to your seat and you don't understand what's going on, you get confused, come back up to the carpet, and we will work on it together." It became a very symbiotic lesson where I just sat on the carpet and worked with kids who needed help. When they thought they knew it, they went back to their seats. If they got confused and didn't know it, they came back to me. I worked with her and demonstrated that it can be done for any lesson. The kids felt valued. The kids felt respected. There was compassion if they needed help. The teacher felt valued and respected by me for having compassion for her by taking the time to work with her. She eventually felt respected by the students because she made the changes necessary to be a high-quality, compassionate teacher.

We shouldn't be expecting kids to know things right away. We're there to facilitate their learning and help them to understand that it's okay not to know. This also pertains to how we teach kids to handle a situation if they hurt someone's feelings. There are a lot of different things that I've seen teachers do where the kids have to go and write what they did and come up with a forced apology. I completely understand that we want kids to apologize for things that have been hurtful. But when we are teaching respect and emotional intelligence, we want to focus on "What did you do wrong? What could you do differently? How could you make this situation better?" If we force an apology, the student is never going to understand what they did wrong or how it was hurtful. Instead, I say, "What did you do wrong? What could you do differently? How could you make this situation better?" I've always had such great success with that one question.

Whether I was a teacher or a principal, I used those questions, and I got the best responses back, and I still do. What can you do to make this better? Some will say, "Oh, I can go apologize." Some will say, "I need to draw a picture." Some will say, "I need to ask that person to play with me on the playground." But when a student generates what *they* can do to make the situation better or what *they* can do differently, that starts building their compassion and their respect level for others, and that's what we want. Sometimes, this is done with much facilitation. Never do I force an apology. I will give suggestions by saying, "Do you want to know what other kids have done?" And then I will give them three suggestions. Helping kids to foster a sense of compassion and empathy for others is a very important life lesson. I also teach kids that when someone apologizes, they don't have to say, "I accept your apology," or "That's okay." I teach kids healthy boundaries by saying, "Thank you for apologizing, but I don't accept your apology," or "Thank you for your apology, but I'm still very hurt," or "I'm still very angry."

As adults, we don't always accept everybody's apology. We can still be angry. We can still be hurt. I facilitate lifelong learning lessons by teaching kids healthy communications, healthy boundaries, and compassion toward others with the hopes that they will become emotionally healthy adults.

EMPOWERMENT

I was working in a middle school in gang territory, and we were told that our sixth grade was going on a district-wide field trip. We were going to go watch the *Nutcracker Ballet*, and I thought, *Oh, no, this could really go wrong in many ways.* Our kids hadn't ever been to a theater, let alone a ballet. They hadn't watched a play or seen an orchestra performance. Having been in dance and theater, I knew some things that could go wrong with the experience: the costumes were the first thing that came to mind, especially the male dancers in tights. I decided *I need to give my students the dignity and respect they deserve and empower them to go to the ballet fully prepared!*

First, my classes conducted research on the story of the Nutcracker so that the students had a clear understanding of what the storyline is. There is no narration or dialogue, and they needed to grasp the storyline to begin to enjoy the ballet. We read various Nutcracker books and various picture books. We compared and contrasted the books. I followed it up with a video of the *Nutcracker Ballet* with Mikhail Baryshnikov. I started by telling them that it's probably going to look like nothing you have ever seen before. We discussed that there would be no dialogue, and the dancers would portray the story through movement. I also stated, "Okay, the male dancers are going to come on stage, and they're going to be wearing tights." I was able to start and stop the video as needed to discuss the story, which they did a pretty great job of. They got that giggling and whooping out of the way while watching the ballet on video. I was able to discuss the pointe shoe, the costumes, and the sets with them. I talked about theater ethics: *When you enter the theater, it's okay to be talking. The theater lights will blink right before the show is about to start. You need to take your seat and be quiet.* We discussed how to clap and show appreciation for a great dance or dance move. The students were so prepared for this event, probably more prepared than some adults are when they go to the ballet. My hope was that when we got into this wonderful cultural setting that they hadn't been in before, they were comfortable, they were confident, and they were respectful. I did everything I could think of to make sure they were empowered to watch this ballet without acting up, while still remembering these were sixth-grade middle schoolers.

They did such a fabulous job. They were the best behaved, in my opinion, and when we got back to the school, we found out that the principal received phone calls from the ballet company and the district office talking about how well-behaved our students were. That was a great caveat for them to be acknowledged for being well-behaved, but more than that, they understood the ballet and the situation we were placing them in, which gave them the empowerment to behave because of their story knowledge and the knowledge of the aspects of a ballet, including the costumes.

We were able to say to the kids, "Hey, guess what? We got phone calls about our school because you all were awesome. You all did such a great job." Did we reward them? Absolutely, but they should have been rewarded because they took the knowledge given to them and demonstrated that they were empowered to watch a ballet in a situation that they were not used to. These are life skills that go beyond the curriculum.

These are the empowerment skills that we need to give to kids. If you're going on a field trip, prepare them for what they're going to experience, not just that they are expected to behave and sit in their seats. What are they going to see? What are they doing? As an adult, if I'm going on a vacation or a trip, I research where I'm going. I know what I want to do and what I want to go see. I research where I'm going before I place myself into a situation.

I challenge educators to place value on empowering students within the learning process. Give them the opportunity to do the research or to talk to them about where they're going, what they're going to see, and what this all is about. We have kids who come from various experiences and backgrounds, and not everybody has a home where they have a lot of experiences. As educators, we need to take time to pre-teach. This doesn't apply only to field trips but to lessons as well. As a special education teacher, I will pre-teach tough concepts to the students on my caseload so that when they are sitting in the larger classroom, they feel confident and successful. I see that the students I work with have blossomed educationally and, most importantly, with confidence. I work as part of an educational team with the teacher whose classroom I work in. Many times, I will pull kids to pre-teach concepts that aren't on my caseload as well. Knowing our students helps to educate and guide them in their learning process at their own abilities. Meet the students where they are and help them rise to the bar. Empower them to be a vital part of the learning process and beyond.

Empowering kids beyond the learning process: What does that look like? I empower students through daily classroom activities to become active decision-makers. "It's time to line up. Do we want to do it in line order or Target style?" "You need to do your work so you can work at the table or at your desk. It's your choice." "It's cold outside. You need to have your coat outside. You can either wear it or carry it during recess." I never give them a choice that is negative. It's always a choice that, in the end, the task is fulfilled. The hope is that even if they make a choice that I wouldn't select, eventually, the better choice will be the outcome. Let's look at the coat issue. If the student chooses not to wear the coat, they must carry it throughout recess. This almost always results in the coat being put on because either they get cold or it becomes a hindrance to their ability to play. When we empower kids in the decision-making process, we begin to foster problem-solving skills, independence, and build a level of confidence and ownership over the decisions they make.

We have to be the facilitators of their learning, the facilitators of helping to empower them to become great people. I'm not going to say great citizens. I'm not going to say great students either, just great humans. Ultimately, it's about getting to know your students, guiding them to what you want them to learn, and then meeting them where they are. That is how I have been an influence on kids. Those students didn't know about the ballet. I had to meet them where they were. Get to know your kids. What do they know? What do they not know? Meet them where they are and provide them with what they need so that they can learn and be successful.

As an administrator and instructional leader, I did the same for teachers. I included them in the decision-making process. When there was a big decision, such as school policies, curriculum changes, or book studies, I talked to teachers individually to get their honest opinions and ideas. I empowered teachers to share in the goals and the decisions of the school. It was *our* school, not my school. I built a strong school culture because teachers were valued, supported, and empowered. Of course, when the final decision was made, if it didn't work out the way we planned, I took full responsibility. That's how I built the safety net for teachers to be empowered to collaborate, present ideas, engage in new classroom strategies, and grow in their educational process. I did daily "walk-throughs" in the school. I would pop in a class for a brief minute or so at various times of the day to see the great things that were happening, and I always tried to follow up with a quick note on their desk or in their mailbox or even a verbal comment later in the day about what I saw. I believe that the teachers felt valued not only as educators but also as people. One summer, I was working on the school schedule. Every time, I would email it to teachers with the statement, "Let me know if you see something that doesn't work." After three times of reworking the schedule, I had a teacher come to me to say that she loves puzzles and scheduling. This was her forte, and would I mind if she worked on the schedule because she had some ideas? I gave it over to her, and she did a fantastic job! When it was presented to the staff, I gave her the acknowledgement for the hard work that she did, but told the teachers that if there were any issues, please see me, and she and I would talk it through. No issues, and this teacher worked on the school schedule every year after. This is just one example of how I found that empowering teachers to share their gifts and knowledge made our school stronger, and the teachers felt valued because they *were* valued, and they had ownership in the school. To this day, I have teachers who contact me to be a job reference for them because they know I valued them as an educator, and they know I could speak to what their classes looked like and felt like, and how they are as people. I have been told by past teachers that I have influenced substitute teachers to finish their degrees, teachers to become principals, and some to further their careers in other ways.

As a principal/instructional leader, I focused on my teachers as educators and collaborators while fostering engaging and respectful learning environments. I tried to instill in my teachers the concept that "You have family first, job second." A principal must value and respect teachers' personal lives. I encouraged teachers to value and respect their own family time, to have that family/work balance so that they could recharge, refocus, and be the best they could be in their family and at the school. I like to consider myself a principal/instructional leader. I believe that the time I spent improving and supporting teachers in their instructional practices, growing great teacher collaborators, and fostering a positive teaching culture was just as important, if not more important, as the day-to-day operational side of the job.

As a teacher, I believe that showing kids they are valued is the biggest influence a teacher can have on kids and families. Making kids feel welcome and important is key. It's all about building positive relationships. For some of our kids, the safest, happiest, and most positive place is being at school. As educators, we must help to foster positive and caring relationships with our kids in our schools. I have many students who feel safe and respected by me, and they open up and tell me about things that happened throughout their day, good or bad, over the weekend, or even their struggles at home. The positive relationships that I foster are genuine. Building respectful bonds with students helps them feel valued, important, and loved. The greatest impact that a teacher can have is not the grades a student gets, but being able to teach kids how to respect others and how to have compassion for others. I am honored to do so. Sometimes we have to put lessons on the back burner, per se, so that we can teach social skills: how to talk, how to listen, and how to have respect and compassion for our classmates.

To work with kids, to teach kids—we are teaching not only the curriculum that is given to us, but also teaching them to be great human beings. As far as teaching them value, respect, compassion, and empowerment, it is part of my classroom every day. I show them that they are valued so that they can show others that value as well. I teach respect and compassion to kids by showing them respect and compassion, by putting respect and compassion into my daily activities, and by adding respect and compassion to my school day, which helps our kids understand what respect and compassion are.

I don't say, "We're going to learn respect; we're going to learn compassion." But that underlying "hidden" curriculum—a tone of respect and compassion—helps our kids become respectful and compassionate students in the school setting, which we hope will carry over into their everyday lives. I empower students to be the best they can possibly be by teaching them the things that go beyond the curriculum, by giving them varied experiences, and by teaching them how to act and react in the experiences. By teaching them to learn from experiences, even if it's something that they have faltered on, we want them to learn from those experiences to be great students and even more awesome humans.

Denise Campbell is an experienced educator and former principal committed to fostering student growth and learning. She focuses on building value and respect while creating engaging, inclusive, and empowering classrooms. Denise also enjoys coaching teachers and principals to help elevate educational practices and leadership.

Denise holds a master's degree focused in Educational Leadership and Administration from Northwest Missouri State University.

To connect with Denise:

—

https://www.linkedin.com/in/denise-campbell-m-ed-educational-leadership-a63b7373/

THE WOMAN WHO CHOSE HERSELF
BY DIANA GARCIA

"We did it!" My mom gave me a big hug and told me we did it. This is one of the single most healing moments I've had in my entire life. I waited years—decades—to have this type of closure. When I made the decision to walk out the door at 16 years old, I carried a lot of guilt for many years—guilt for leaving my siblings and for not knowing what was happening to them. I would call the house to remind my father that at any point, I could send him to jail. I traveled the world and got wined and dined while my family was still in poverty. These are all things that I've had to heal from, beyond the physical wounds from years of abuse and the hand marks that were so deeply imprinted into my soul.

The journey of healing isn't about forgiving others; it's about feeling good and being proud of who you are today, despite what you've gone through or the decisions you've made. I've noticed that those who have an unshakable desire to help others, most of us have a story to tell—a story that's taken years to tell and years to heal from. The journey begins at birth; I came out into this world in a hurry, a couple of months premature, but grew to mature into someone who fully understands her purpose. I remember wondering why I was born, and my father reminded me of that question all the time.

I started sleepwalking at the age of four or five. I was in kindergarten, and instead of playing with the other kids, I questioned why I was having these horrible episodes where all I wanted to do was escape. These sleepwalking episodes caused my entire family to have many sleepless nights, and let's just say I wasn't the favorite child.

The locks had to be moved up so that I couldn't reach them; otherwise, I'd have ended up outside at 3 a.m. But was that a safer place? When I was 7, I learned how to stand up for my mother without fear—I stood in front of her so that he wouldn't touch her. Like clockwork, in the middle of the night, the shouting would begin, and my duty to protect her began. It was a 3 a.m. shift that nobody wanted, but I felt like it was my calling to do so. He never touched her—at least we never saw him touch her. Instead, I became the human punching bag. At first, it started with hand marks, then it led to being struck with objects; the final blow was a punch to the face.

There were many moments in my life where I just did not want to be there; I had to really fight all of those feelings, but I didn't understand why I was a target, constantly being attacked. My family recalls some of the moments they felt the safest were when I was in front of them, standing between them and my father, and not letting him touch them. School became my escape because anywhere felt safer than being at home. All of my teachers were amazing; they seemed to instinctively know that something was off without knowing exactly what it was. The German teacher, whose class I would crash in my free period, would pull me aside and ask if I was alright. I would answer with "Yes, I'm okay." Technically, I wasn't lying, because while I was at school, I was okay. I loved being at school and did everything possible to stay at school as long as possible every day.

At age 12, I experienced one of the most pivotal moments in my life. At this point, I had endured many years of physical, verbal, and emotional abuse. The beatings didn't stop. I didn't understand why they were happening; I just knew that I couldn't sit back and do nothing. So I stood in front of my mother and sisters and resumed my role as the primary punching bag. At this point, we had lived in at least eight homes, and I had gone to eight different schools. We got a phone call one day that my uncle went to jail, and my mom said, "We have to go be near him. Let's pack up and go." So we moved from Austin to Indiana, right outside my hometown of Chicago—the place my soul felt most connected to. When my uncle went to jail, I wanted to be in the courtroom as much as my mom would let me. In that courtroom, I saw so much injustice from the prosecution team. I did countless hours of research and wondered what it would be like to be his lawyer. His lawyers didn't seem to fight; they did not defend and seemed to be defeated by the prosecution team. I witnessed this long battle with my uncle, and I couldn't do anything about it as a 12-year-old, but the experience fueled me to want to be a lawyer. This gave me a mission and a purpose and ultimately a focus to distract myself from the abuse that was happening at home. It gave me a very clear roadmap, as there were specific things I needed to do to get into law school. That included not getting into any trouble, being a straight-A student, and doing a lot of community service. *Spoiler alert:* I didn't end up being a lawyer. I really wanted to, though—not just get into law school and become a lawyer, but to become the best of the best. My mission became clear: I would go to Harvard, I would share my story with them, and they would accept me with a full-ride scholarship. This was what I aimed for and what I was manifesting. Little did I know that I had an even greater mission. This was just the pathway for now.

I knew that I wanted to help people. And as much as I couldn't help my uncle, perhaps I could channel that desire into helping others. With this pursuit of wanting to go to law school, I actually did end up talking to Harvard, and they gave me some really good advice. They said I would have to be extremely well-rounded and do things in the community. It gave me a really clear roadmap of the things that I needed to do, but it also gave me a really good distraction from what was happening at home. I spent minimal time at home. And if you saw me in school or out at a community or sporting event, I was so happy not to have to deal with the chaos or the mood swings or the violence. I was zoned in and determined. No one could tell me that I wasn't going to be a lawyer.

My plan was clear: I was going to go to Harvard, and I was on that path. But at 16, I received an answer to a prayer. I knew something really bad would have to happen for me to leave home before I turned 18—I knew I couldn't continue to endure the violence much longer, and graduating and leaving for Harvard seemed a lifetime away. When it happened, I knew it was the moment that I had been praying for, but still, I wasn't prepared. I was standing in the kitchen on the phone one day, and out of nowhere, I was punched in the face. The left side of my jaw, to be exact. I remember looking at the door—it felt like minutes went by with me standing there, calm, but hesitating about my next move. My therapy team advised me that it was probably less than sixty seconds, but it felt like much longer. I remember feeling like I was at a crossroads and asking myself, *Do I leave and leave my siblings? Or do I stay and continue the abuse?* If I stayed. I feared something much worse would happen next. I realized that this was the moment I had prayed for. So I walked out the door, and I never looked back.

I walked for miles; I remember feeling that if I turned back and saw my father or my siblings, I wouldn't have been able to leave. I would've had to walk back and stay. So I didn't turn around. Instead, I hurried to the end of the street, running part of the way. I kept my focus on the path forward. This became such a symbolic moment for me in my life: Whenever I'm at a crossroads, or something intense is happening, I just tell myself, *I did it. I can do anything because I did the hard thing.* Leaving my home at 16, walking for miles to my mom's job—all of my plans went out the window. So now what?

I had prepared so much for this moment in whatever way I could as a teenager—my preparation to be a lawyer had given me access to all the legal entities to be emancipated and all of the rights that I had, including any support that I could get from the government. But I had never considered what would happen on the exact day that I left. Where would I run to? Where would I live? Now what? I had to let it all go, and I fully surrendered. I trusted in a bigger plan and a divine path. At this moment, I became fully in tune with my intuition, and because of this moment, I knew how to tap into and guide myself through the next few decades of my life. Ultimately, I learned the art of allowing, and I learned that boundaries are really good. These are all realizations that I didn't have in that exact moment, but I knew that I deserved better, and I knew that it was out there. I just needed to take the first step.

At 16, I was forced to be more responsible than I've ever been. I felt like I always had responsibilities growing up, from doing chores to helping my mom make extra money. We would often make tamales with her or create little gadgets that we could sell for food or supplies we needed for school. My mom always found opportunities and made everything possible. We didn't have a lot of money. Some days, I didn't even know how we were going to have food on the table. I'm so thankful for food pantries, churches, and government assistance. But I never thought that I would be homeless on my own with no one to run to. A lot of people asked me what happened next, and the only thing I can share is that I went to stay with my friend for a few days. I went into freeze mode and shock. But like my true resilient self, I trusted. I don't remember really ever crying. I didn't have time to grieve. I just had time to focus on the path forward.

I was a big dreamer, and I still had this big dream to go to Harvard. But I felt like things got a little bit more complicated. I knew deep down inside that life was going to be incredible from here on out because I chose myself.

People are always very curious as to the timeline and the exact things that I did upon leaving my home. I was a little girl who didn't know exactly what to do. I didn't even have a cell phone. Reliving these exact moments is not good for my mental health, and this is why I'm writing this chapter and my full book. I'm ready to move on. And I'm hopeful that this will help someone who may find themselves in a similar situation. Family repair and healing are possible.

My first step was to find a safe place to live. Most of my family decided not to take me in. They said they didn't want to get involved. I was forced to make a decision to move outside of my school district, and thankfully, my grandmother on my mom's side said that I could live with her until I figured things out. I was really close with my administrators; I let them know what happened, and they did everything possible to keep me in the same high school. They are my angels. They knew that my dream was still to go to Harvard, and changing schools one more time would complicate things even further. On top of that, I was class president, student council vice president, and had won so many awards. One day, I got the idea to use my mom's information to apply for an apartment in Chicago–Montrose Harbor, to be exact. I called my mom and said, "Well, I just used your information, and I hope that you're okay with that. I applied for an apartment." Thankfully, she said that if it goes through, just do it. We both prayed! I didn't have any doubts, and thankfully it went through. So at 16, I had an apartment in my mom's name, and that's the reference to the beginning of this chapter. We did it. We both had to have blind faith. And there it began: complete independence and the ability to make every decision on my own.

I couldn't believe how much toilet paper costs! So, how was I ever going to pay rent? I needed to get a couple of jobs. Prior to the final blow, in my quest to be a lawyer, I had learned that I could actually get money from the government. Whatever the situation was, I knew exactly how to apply to get a monthly benefit. It still wasn't enough for all of my bills, rent, and all the food that my friends would eat because they were all excited that I had my own place. And then my friend decided to get us tickets to go see our favorite band, Linkin Park. I'd never been to a concert, but music had been in my life since I was born. My dad was a musician; He was extremely successful before I was born. And when I was born, he decided to go into music ministry. I was surrounded by instruments, and my dad even made me sing in church. I didn't enjoy music, and I didn't enjoy singing. Because of his newfound religious views, he did not let us listen to secular music. He didn't know that Linkin Park had become my favorite band. Here we were going to our first concert, and not only that, we were going to see my favorite band. On the day of the show, we found out that we were going to meet them! This wasn't just any concert; it was Ozzfest. Can you imagine two young 16-year-old girls, one of whom was living on her own, going to this festival?! When we got to the meet and greet, we decided to stand at the back of the line, thinking perhaps we'd get more time with them, and we were right.

While we were standing in line and waiting, I met some people from their label. They asked us a bunch of questions, like what part of town we lived in, whether we liked going to concerts, and if we were looking for any opportunities to go to more concerts. They knew we were young, but thankfully, they never asked our age. Looking back, they assumed that we were in college. We presented ourselves as mature and very composed. I did not want to act like a superfan, even though deep down inside, I was so excited to meet my favorite band. By the time we got up to the band, I basically had a job in hand. I was offered a few opportunities, one of those being a field rep for Warner Bros. and helping them at shows in Chicago. They felt like it was a perfect alignment because I lived in the city and could access any show as well as do anything in the city, like work with the record stores to make displays. They loved that I lived in the city! They also appreciated that I loved all of the artists on Warner Bros. at the time. I knew their entire roster and could talk about it for endless hours. At the moment, I thought it was super ironic because I didn't know a ton about labels.

This was my first really big opportunity and the first moment that I can recall when I was at the right place at the right time. I can tell you that at that moment, I did not think that this would be my entire career and that it would take me all over the world; I just knew that I had to say yes, and saying yes felt so fun and exciting. Getting paid to go to concerts? How fun is that?! If I left my home and my siblings, I was going to have so much fun and just make the most out of this.

In the back of my mind, I knew I was going to be successful, but I always thought it would be as a lawyer. I never gave up on that vision. I knew that one day I was going to bring abundance into my family's life, and I was going to help my siblings. I've had this unshakable desire for something so much greater, and I've had this dreamer-like instinct since I was born. I tell people all the time, I was just so ready to enter this world—two months early, to be exact. And that's the attitude that I had from that day moving forward. I was going to make the most of everything. My plans could pivot, and they could change, but if it was leading me to working with my favorite band, then everything was working out. I was now working in the music industry with one of the biggest labels in the entire world. I was meeting some of the most powerful people in the music industry. I always had this demeanor of professionalism that allowed me to enter rooms that no one else could enter. I sat at dinner tables with some of the most powerful people, and everyone just told me how professional I was. I look back to when I was 12 and when I was in that courtroom; that taught me a lot about how I should talk and how I should act. I took those things seriously, and focusing on that business professionalism also kept me from making mistakes that others might have, things like channeling my pain into substance abuse, running off with a partner, or straying away from my faith. In these moments, my faith grew stronger, and I kept really strict boundaries.

As a teenager living on my own, who had hardly any contact with my family, I knew the odds were against me. But I chose joy. I chose to start a career. I knew that I needed to solidify myself in something because no one was going to be there to save me. Living in Chicago was honestly so much easier than pursuing the opportunity to go to Harvard and become a lawyer. I chose the easier path, and let me tell you, it's been so much fun. As I reflect on the past two decades of being in the music industry, I'm so grateful for every human who has entered my life. They inadvertently protected me. Ninety-nine percent of the artists that I have worked with have been so kind and respectful towards me. Most, but not all, of the people that I have encountered in the ministry have respected me. For many years, not one person knew what had happened to me. I was even invited to celebrate Thanksgiving with Madonna's family. I politely declined because I was so emotionally distraught by the idea of being around another family. But everyone who surrounded me kept trying to include me in their lives.

Linkin Park and their music really saved my life. Warner Bros. Records also saved my life, and the three wise men (as I call them—Larry, Dave, and Bob) changed my life forever with their support, their compassion, and their willingness to give me opportunities. They had no idea of the pain I was still dealing with: My jaw was still messed up from the punch to the face (it would lock constantly), the hand marks on my body that were so deeply imprinted, I had the feeling of abandonment like I didn't have a family anymore, and I had the pain of not knowing what was happening back home.

I was able to mask the internal pain and abandonment throughout most of my career. But I think a lot of people knew there was something else going on, and they surrounded me like beautiful angels, putting me in some really fun and outrageous situations that many people don't get in their lifetime. Getting to hang out with Muse and take them to the Green Mill, gambling with Taking Back Sunday in Vegas, sitting next to Flea on the ground listening to their entire album *Stadium Arcadium,* and countless times standing in an empty arena feeling like I was a part of something bigger. I'm really grateful for entering this industry, being adopted, and also having them witness my growth, transformation, and healing.

Throughout the years, I've been so open to learning, and that has really helped me in this last part of my healing journey. I felt like a sponge: "Tell me! Show me! Let's do it all." Warner Bros. really gave me that expansion. When I was 19, they offered me the opportunity to go to Los Angeles to work for their office. I'd graduated from high school, started college, and decided to stay in Chicago and not go to Harvard. Harvard was still possible, but this new path was just way too exciting. Everyone had received me with open arms, and that felt really good. After a summer on the Warped Tour, breaking up My Chemical Romance, I decided to say yes to the offer and go out to LA and start this next chapter in my career.

When I moved to LA, I dove into work and felt so blessed with the creative opportunity to do anything and everything I ever could have dreamed of. But this was a distraction. I knew that if I tapped into the hurt and the pain, it would take me down, and I wasn't ready for that. I had the conscious awareness that at some point I was going to have to face it: face my reality, face the pain, face the day that I left, but now was not the time. During my time in LA, I had back-to-back massive number-one albums. I led some of the biggest album releases to date. I relaunched Madonna's career. I relaunched the Red Hot Chili Peppers' career and became friends with them. I kept working with some of my favorite artists. It was a really unbelievable time in my career, but all I could think about was that I had a dream, and my dream was to have my family. To have moments with my mother. To get my family out of poverty. To find healing. To understand why my father was so abusive. While everyone around me was paving a path for my career, every day I would think about not giving up on that dream and making sure that it was possible. In all honesty, I didn't care about my career. I didn't care about the number ones. I didn't care about the praise. I didn't care about any of those things, and because I didn't care, this is why I became so successful. I was just in the flow. I understood how to follow my intuition. I understood how to channel success, and it became really easy for me. The big things were really easy. Having a relationship with my family was still really hard. Thinking about being around my father was painful. My body rejected it. I got sick every time I went to visit my family. Healing was not the easy path. My career was an easy path. I could have taken the easy path, given up on healing and repairing the relationships with people who abused me and hurt me really badly. But I had a dream. My spirit told me to never give up.

I didn't know that healing would take many years of trial and error, but it ultimately brought me to the place where my dreams came true. Every time I felt like I was ready to either have the conversation with my family or figure out ways we could all heal together, it was denied.

Healing can't really be done as a group effort. It has to be done individually, and I knew that it had to start with me. I knew that I had to start opening up about all of the abuse and not shut down, and most importantly, I knew I needed to forgive myself for leaving that day. The real healing began during COVID. Like most people, we don't ever want to relive that period of time. I ended up having five family members die in two years from COVID, and each death opened up the conversation for my family to reconnect.

Although these deaths are extremely painful and can be sometimes numbing, they have brought so much healing into my family's lives because we are now closer than ever. Sometimes tragedy has a way of opening the door to conversations. The conversations didn't flow, and they didn't necessarily open up right away, but through the support of my therapy team and through the support of a book that I was reading, I was able to address certain things with my family and pick up the phone and have a conversation. We had many hours of conversation, and I finally had the opportunity to ask questions that I had always wanted to ask. Those questions weren't always answered immediately, but at least we could think about them and reconnect when we all felt comfortable. My uncle Santiago was the last family member to die in that season. He was the first and only one on my mom's side to pass away from COVID. To tie it all together, he's the one who went to jail when I was 12.

I had a really hard time grappling with it all because it seemed so unfair that someone who had been sentenced to twenty years in prison had now died from COVID. It was tough. All deaths are hard, but this one just didn't make sense to me. Some days are still more difficult than others.

My uncle's death allowed my mom and me to have some of the closest moments we've ever had. It allowed that little girl, my younger self, to have moments like sleepovers, hugs, and I love you's that I really never got as a kid. My uncle brought us together again. I would do anything to have him here with us, but we both recognized that it was his time, and his death was just the next step in his life's path. He's at peace, and certainly his presence is felt. His death prompted my mom and me to move forward, not only wanting a relationship but also acting on it.

My career started off with my favorite band, which would end up being one of the biggest bands in the entire world, Linkin Park. It led to so many opportunities with other artists and ultimately has helped me to launch my own business. I have an agency where I now get to pick who I want to work with and what I want to do. I have experienced moments that people wish for. Moments that are magical. I do have moments where I sit back and just shake my head and say out loud, "What an incredible life I've been given." I live in gratitude every single day, and I take every opportunity as a beautiful blessing in my life. And I treat my clients that way.

A lot of times, people want to introduce me as someone who has worked with these big-name artists. "Diana ... She's worked with Madonna and Rascal Flatts." Most of the time, I try to push that off because I want to be known for the fact that I have such a beautiful gift to lift people out of tough seasons in their lives. By learning to do the impossible within my career, I also learned how to lift people up out of their darkest hour. I would always go back and remember the days when I was in the courtroom with my uncle and sit there and just think, *This isn't fair.* And so I've always been one to fight for justice and to stand in front of anyone who was a victim of injustice. A lot of people say, "Diana, you're very successful." And for a while, I had a really hard time grappling with that because I didn't feel successful.

I finally realized that this feeling of inadequacy was because I defined success as moments with my family, feeling whole, feeling great, knowing that I chose myself, and that was the best decision I have ever made. But I never gave up on my dream.

A couple of years ago, I was at church, and I had one of the most powerful moments I have ever had in my life. Growing up, my father was a Pentecostal preacher, and most people in my position would have abandoned the church. I actually embraced it even more when I moved out of my house. On this day, the preacher was talking about surrender. I cried the entire service. There have been very few sermons in my whole life that I have cried the entire time. I was sitting there two decades later from the moment I left my house, and for the entire service, I was talking to God and saying, "I don't know how to surrender. I've had this amazing career, but I don't know how to let go of these fears of homelessness, fears of messing up, fears of no one being there for me. Teach me how to surrender."

When you move out on your own at such a young age, there are a lot of things that you need to learn. In this moment, I really wanted to surrender the perfectionism, the worry, and the doubt. My life was okay and always has been. My life was great, but there was something inside of me that was still broken. I knew at this moment that I had to go back home, and I needed to reevaluate my life once more. It took me back to the time when I was 16 and walked out the door without a plan. So why did I feel like this time I needed to have a plan? I've coached people through something that's called going back to zero. I've done this a few times, and at this moment, this was the second time that I was going to take myself to zero. I knew that if I did that, I would be able to really find healing. Going to zero means you have no identity, and you just focus on the things that make you happy.

For two decades, my identity was in my career, and I really wanted something more. I decided that I wanted to do exactly what I said I was going to do when I walked out that door. That was to go and help people. Throughout my music career, I have talked to millions of people and millions of fans whose lives have been impacted by lyrics. I've sat with so many fans as they've cried and said, "This music saved my life." Music saved my life, too. So I wanted to build a brand where I was truly living out my purpose and building a legacy. What would I be known for? Would I be known for helping Madonna get her first number-one album? Or would I be known for the millions of people I can help? So I launched my brand, House of Darlings. I wanted everything to be rooted in helping others and also having fun. House of Darlings isn't just a thread; it's a movement and inspires others to believe that they can change the world. I was on probably what would be my second sabbatical, and I asked myself this question: *What can I do every day that would be so fun that I could enjoy life and build a brand around it?* And I remembered that there were moments when I would go over to my grandfather's house and hear the roaring sounds of his sewing machines. He was a tailor. He made suits. I only spent a year with him before he passed away. This was just a year after we had moved back, when my uncle had gone to jail. In that one year, he sparked so much inside of me, including this desire to be in fashion. My mom also inspired me in so many ways. She would sew my sister and me two-piece sets because we couldn't afford to go shopping. I wish so badly that I still had those two-piece sets.

This internal desire to be in fashion didn't come until two decades later, when I decided that I wanted to find my purpose. So, in this moment of waking up and feeling like I wanted to do what would make me so happy every day and do something that could also help people, I connected the dots, and I decided to launch my first fashion collection. And because of that first fashion collection, we were able to send foster youth on a shopping spree. This collection started my journey of impacting people all over the world. I somehow landed in Uganda and was able to fundraise to open up a maternity ward in Kikum, Uganda. And that's single-handedly one of the most special moments I'll ever have in my life. Being able to stand in the maternity ward and walk around with a doctor and see how babies were going to be born here, free of HIV and AIDS. It gave me meaning. It gave me so much more purpose beyond the music I was promoting. But everything I had done in my career had led me to these experiences so that I could build something to influence others to live out their legacy and help others.

Throughout the past ten years, since launching House of Darlings, I've been able to help over 100,000 women and kids. And I'm so excited about what's next because I have a big mission and I have a big goal in mind. The difference between me now and then is that I've forgiven myself, and I'm ready to share my story because your dreams really can come true. And a lot of times, we think our dreams are a certain status in a career, a job title, a car, or a home. I've had all those things, and I've helped a lot of people get those things. But I'm really interested in what your real dream is. I'm so proud of myself that I never gave up. There were so many times when it was really hard, and I had to take a pause on pursuing a relationship with my family. But this entire journey has led us to not just making up for lost time but also building new memories that feel like recollections that we would have had when I was younger. I recently got to take my mom to Paris on her dream trip. A client called me and said they wanted to send me to Portugal. And then I called my mom and said, "Well, we're stopping in Paris first, and you're coming with me."

We got to sit in front of the Eiffel Tower, and we got to say it again: "We did it." It was our second biggest major manifestation that we did together, and we were able to do it from a healed place. My journey is not over, and yours isn't either. I hope that my message and a glimpse inside my life give you hope that you can have it all and you can do it all. Little by little, step by step, you're going to get there. Just don't give up. Okay?

Diana Garcia is a visionary strategist, a creative force, and now an author. Often referred to as a secret weapon, she has mobilized millions of fans across the globe while working with artists who've moved economies and shaped culture. Her campaigns with icons like Rascal Flatts, Madonna, Dolly Parton, Linkin Park, My Chemical Romance, Muse, and Coldplay helped launch some of the highest-selling albums of recent decades, pioneering the rise of super-fan communities in the digital age.

Today, Diana channels her influence into her most personal and powerful venture yet: House of Darlings. More than a fashion brand, it's a movement—one that threads purpose into every stitch and initiative. With several collections launched and over ten philanthropic campaigns funded—including shopping sprees for children in foster care, sending soldiers home for Christmas, supporting cancer patients, and providing clean water in Africa—House of Darlings is redefining what it means to lead with heart.

In 2025, Diana steps into a new chapter as an author, sharing her testimony through multiple book projects that explore healing, resilience, and radical self-worth. Her debut contribution, *Limitless Impact,* features her chapter "The Woman Who Chose Herself"—a raw and empowering reflection on identity, boundaries, and rebirth.

Her upcoming collection, Rebirth, launches alongside her book and is designed to make a lasting impact on women and children worldwide. With over 100,000 lives already touched, Diana's mission is clear: to inspire others to believe in their own power to choose themselves, rise again, and change the world.

LIMITLESS IMPACT

To connect with Diana:

—

https://bio.site/dianagarcia

—

www.instagram.com/dianagarcia

—

https://www.tiktok.com/@houseofdarlings

—

http://www.instagram.com/houseofdarlings

K.I.S.S. CODEPENDENCY GOODBYE: KEEP IT SIMPLE & SCIENTIFIC

BY EILEEN SAKOFSKY

In the spring of 2011, my husband spent $12,000 on crack, prostitutes, and seedy motel rooms... *In one month.*

Unless you have lived with an addict or abuser, it's hard to understand the implications of what life is like when someone *whom you love* is one and how radically it can f*ck with your head.

I have never been an addict, but addiction dramatically changed the course of my life.

I wasn't a drinker or a drug user. What I had become was an excruciatingly frustrated, angry, stressed-out, heartbroken, desperate, needy, stuck young woman whose life and personal identity were consumed and defined by the demented needs and attitudes of an addict. I lost sight of better judgment about what I was worth, what I should not put up with, and what belief structure I had been operating in. But I never gave up on myself.

I was the gatekeeper who tried desperately to keep him from going on his insane, insatiable quest to get high. I became the adversary trying to stop it and, therefore, the recipient of all the darkness from the heart of a person whose view on life had become skewed from drug abuse. He was once beautiful, adventurous, charismatic, goofy, smart, and had a very big heart. He had this larger-than-life persona and magnetic energy. It's pretty damning to your psyche when you alternately go from being beloved to being called a "f*cking stupid, worthless, dumbass, piece of shit bitch," and much worse.

I was so invested in him and this unrealistic idea that I could love him enough to save him—*and our life together*—that it took me down a long 30-year road of codependency and abuse that eventually led to me being homeless with kids, having to live with family and friends, and in and out of hotels and motels for many years.

Many, many times I thought to myself, *Why am I trying so desperately to save something that I have come to despise so deeply?*

Looking back, it's hard to even comprehend what *I allowed* to adversely affect my life for so many years.

Nevertheless, I vehemently oppose the label "codependent," as it represents an agreement with yourself—a declaration of ownership over an identity. Codependent behaviors and actions are not inherent traits; they are belief systems, mindsets, and habit patterns that can be changed. When you label your identity, you are proclaiming who you are and how you perceive yourself. So be wise in your choice of labels, as your identity shapes your actions, and your actions, in turn, become self-fulfilling.

I emerged *not* as a survivor, but as someone determined to create lasting change.

I want to encourage you that *no matter what you have been through*, whether it's due to having an addicted spouse or just being so entrenched in your own limiting, maladaptive beliefs ingrained from earlier life experiences that your well-being, fulfillment, and joy are suffering, you can rewrite your own powerful new story without letting negative narratives be the author.

I want you to understand that you already possess the inherent tools within yourself to come through it as a wiser, stronger, more self-reliant, intentional, confident, happier, next-best version of yourself—one that can and *should* be progressively and continually improved.

My chapter in *Limitless Impact* is a testament to resilience, resourcefulness, and the power of vision and intentionality. My journey has been one of painful yet purposeful lessons, teaching me the following: obstacles are not barriers but opportunities for growth; you must take ownership of, learn from, and then give yourself grace to move beyond your most regrettable mistakes; success is not about resources but your resourcefulness; finding gratitude for the things in your life, *no matter how messed up of a state that it may be in,* is foundational in keeping your life in perspective, joyful, and open for expansion; and perseverance is key to transformation. Even when your best-laid plans seem to fail, which many of mine did, you can be empowered to keep learning, challenging yourself, and figuring it out! Keep figuring *you* out! The best and *only* way to become a confident person is to show up for yourself, do the hard things, and persevere until you get there. Know that you can rely on *you*. When progress feels slow or setbacks seem insurmountable, remember to give yourself credit for the *effort* that you are making to make your life better! Every *effort* brings you closer to your defining moment. I am living proof that success is not a destination but a journey, and on that journey, you may learn things and have opportunities present themselves to you that you never thought possible.

And it simply starts with a vision, a decision, and a declaration of who you want to be.

As far back as I can remember, even in the midst of the chaos when my life was in complete shambles, I *knew* that I was going to be an author to tell my story to inspire other women, and I was relentlessly intentional about it. As unrealistic as that seemed to some, I believed it.

It has taken me a very long time to get here, but what's even more astounding about actually accomplishing it is the information that I have learned along the way. *Never, ever* in my wildest dreams could I have imagined that I would learn about and leverage the knowledge of neuroscience. My whole journey is about change, and what I have learned is that our brains have unimaginable abilities to rewire their connections, to build new neural pathways... and to change. It's called *neuroplasticity.*

Getting a snapshot of my journey will give you an understanding of how I got to the amazing discovery that I feel like I have been bestowed with the privilege, and really the *responsibility,* to be the conduit of the life-changing information that you might not ever have heard otherwise.

So it was that as I attempted to go down the traditional roads of "recovery," I realized that they were not the path for me.

K.I.S.S. CODEPENDENCY GOODBYE: KEEP IT SIMPLE & SCIENTIFIC

THERAPY

Therapy is definitely right for some. It can help you to find clarity in things that you may not have considered, constructively help to sort out your feelings, and teach you strategies to deal with them. That said, however, it's not the path that I took. To be honest, I just didn't want to.

Inner child work had become popular in the 1990s, was all the rage back then, and is a valuable path of discovery for many. But I had a pretty clear understanding of my past. I was a child of the '60s and '70s. I had an idyllic life in the Catskill Mountains with my parents and my brothers. I had grandparents, aunts, uncles, and cousins whom I loved. But we lived very close to Woodstock, which my parents attended on the last day... *And then everything changed.* They became hippies and then got divorced. My mom, an accomplished classical pianist—hailing from the famous High School of Music and Performing Arts—did a gutsy thing and traveled west on a journey of self-discovery, and when I was only in the fifth grade, I moved with her far away from the rest of my family to Cocolalla, Idaho. My dad, a Brown-educated Sigma Nu fraternity brother, went from being a prominent small-town New York Jewish attorney to becoming a Christian truck driver, masseur, carpenter/craftsman, and blissful "ski bum." The solidarity and peacefulness of driving big rigs cross-country were freeing for him. He eventually moved to Killington, Vermont, building houses in the summer and in winter merrily skiing his days away and being the resident masseur at the lodge in the evenings for many years. This life suited him better than the suits of an attorney ever could have.

But there were large swaths of time that I didn't see my dad, brothers, or the rest of my family, *which no doubt influenced my desire to keep my own marriage and family together.* My childhood had become a mixed bag of divorce, disruption, separation, and sadness that I dealt with for many years. But it was also infused with the influence of the peace, love, rock 'n' roll, and deep-breathing massage therapy movement, which we had become part of. My kind, gentle dad became an example of learning to be happy in life as your authentic self, and he was the first to introduce me to the concept of faith. My mom had also become a massage therapist, studied Tai Chi under the great Al Huang, and was pictured in one of his books. A friend of hers challenged me to memorize the Desiderata: "Go placidly amid the noise and the haste, and remember what peace there may be in silence."

Knowing what I know now, I believe I had formed some very deeply ingrained beliefs that, although excruciating pain happens, you can also experience extraordinary beauty in the midst of it.

I just didn't feel like I had a wounded inner child.

I remember thinking, *I have already lived through and know all of the pains that have led me to this point in my life.* How was focusing on the pains of my past going to help move me into the future? For me personally, it wasn't, so I didn't adhere to that theory of therapy.

As a teenager, I happened to have been extremely blessed to have learned some deeply insightful wisdom from one of the world's most extraordinary people. We had moved to San Diego, and my mom worked for a company where she met the then-young, up-and-coming Tony Robbins, who became a family friend. He deeply impressed upon me that I had the personal power within myself to choose how the circumstances of life would have their effect on me and the belief that I am the one in control of the way I choose to perceive them. He taught me the importance of being intentional, and looking back, I can clearly see that was a guiding principle on my journey. I learned what personal development was from him, which eventually changed my entire life. I didn't always heed his wisdom, but it helped shape my belief system, and I never forgot it.

As Tony Robbins says, "The past does not equal the future, unless you live there." I knew that I did not want to continue to live there. I just didn't know how to get to where I wanted to be… *yet.*

THE 12 STEPS OF AL-ANON

I very quickly determined that the 12-step *ideology and methodology* were not for me. The steps to help the family are exactly the same as those for the addict; although "codependency" encompasses a different set of issues, it is offered the same system of solutions. They instruct us to believe that a power greater than ourselves could restore our sanity and to profess the exact nature of our "wrongdoing, shortcomings, and defects in character" to that power. Restore *our* sanity. Admit *our* wrongdoing. Remove *our* defects of character. Praying *only for knowledge of His* will.

Faith and humbly seeking God for clarity, guidance, and wisdom were not new to me. Having a spiritual connection had already been a vital part of my life. I had been going to church for many years, attended Bible studies and women's groups, and was doing my best to be a "Proverbs 31 wife."

However, these steps sat wrong in my spirit, and my head was screaming... *WTF?*

We all have shortcomings and should all have good standing in our own moral inventory. However, those steps seemed to implicitly presuppose that we are inherently defective.

I understand there are nuanced interpretations to the steps, but reading them at face value, that is a core tenet of this system.

In my experience, when contemplating what the steps implied and the strategy of embodying them deeply and adhering to them as truth, it just didn't resonate with me. Not only did I not believe that philosophy, but I had landed at this meeting because of the destruction in my life that was caused by *my husband's* drinking, drugging, lying, cheating, stealing, neglect, and abuse... All stemming from *his insanity*, not mine.

I'd had enough of being told by my husband that I was wrong, defective, and not good enough when I knew that wasn't true. The 12 steps seemed to deepen the subconscious mindset of being "not good enough" that most women develop when they have an addicted spouse.

Although the purpose of this program is to help you gain back your sense of self-identity, self-worth, and stability in your own life, working on steps to accomplish that by continually meditating on admitting defectiveness didn't seem like a viable way to build personal power and not an approach I was even willing to try.

Besides the steps, just the meeting itself, I was like, *Whoa... What have I walked into?* I heard people refer to their "Q" which I didn't know what that was but came to learn that it meant my "qualifier." My husband *qualified* me to be there. Huh, weird. *(Again, I know... nuanced meaning, it's meant as a term for privacy... but still, weird.)*

I was like, *Cool, I am now qualified to be a part of the Codependent Wife of an Addict club.* And when I learned the term "Old Timers," some of whom were still with their "Q" and even some who had long left the relationship with their "Q" but were still coming to the meetings many years after, still sitting around talking about it... I couldn't even imagine that being my new reality and future.

It all felt like a weirdly programmed, cultish club. I knew that was *definitely* not what I wanted my life to look like, not the identity that I wanted to maintain, or the environment that I wanted to be part of.

PASTORAL COUNSELING

The final breaking point was when a pastor who was counseling me asked, "What is your sin in the situation?" *Excuse me?* I thought. *MY sin?!*

I never claimed to be perfect, but I was a faithful wife trying my best to have some sort of a normal life, while my husband was an out-of-control drug addict who constantly cheated on me and did many other unimaginably destructive, heartbreaking things. And this pastor had the audacity to ask me what *my* sin was in this situation!

I am filled with gratitude for the many people whom I encountered *at* church over the years. However, I came to the realization that the church was not the answer that was going to lead me to the changes that I was seeking.

Women all around the world, from all classes, races, and spiritual beliefs, struggle with addicted, abusive men and their toxicity. It's insanely easy to lose yourself in the vortex of madness... no matter how smart or even how successful you are.

You agonize over breaking your vows and tearing your families apart, yet are filled with self-loathing agony for allowing it to become paramount to your own well-being, personal identity, confidence, and quality of life. You find yourselves living in patterns of self-doubt and brokenness, in survival mode, doing everything that you can think of to try to get it under control. Codependency becomes a programmed pattern that you are so used to operating in that it just becomes the norm of who you are and how you live. And then, like pouring salt into your wounds, you are led to believe that because of your learned and programmed maladaptive beliefs, behavioral patterns of codependent habits, and neurochemical feedback loops, that you have a *defect in your character* and are *full of sin* because of it.

How utterly misinformed we have been.

I knew that I needed to find a more positive, universal solution. I also knew that there were—and still are—many women who do not believe in God in any understanding and who have no desire to be instructed to do so, yet are still seeking solutions. I just didn't know what the answers were... *yet*.

As catastrophic as things had become over the years, though, I was able to stay true to the core of who I am: a naturally happy, easygoing, curious, glass-three-quarters-to-overflowing outlook kind of girl. I never gave up on the *vision* of what I wanted my life to be. That vision propelled me to take all sorts of *actions* toward becoming the person I *believed* I could be and attaining the life that I yearned to live... despite the seemingly insurmountable obstacles I was dealing with. As a result of the *determined* but sometimes seemingly futile actions that I kept taking, I also experienced many incredible, awe-inspiring, amazing things.

Everything, and I mean all of it, was part of the process of progress. But with little to no results to help me figure out how to change my life *yet*, I went on a journey of self-discovery and personal growth and development that eventually led me to research the workings of our minds.

It was in January of 2008 when I came across an ad in the *San Diego Union-Tribune:* "Online Fitness Coaches Needed, No Experience Necessary." I had been doing aerobics since I was 17 years old and was an avid power walker, so I thought that this might be right up my alley.

I had never heard anything quite like what I was hearing at this meeting. I was completely captivated. It wasn't the business model that I was so enthralled with, though; it was the business of *changing people's lives.*

When the meeting was over, I was the very last person left in the room talking to the presenters, Julie and Bill Wainer. I knew that I wanted to be involved.

This is where my transformation truly began. Julie, Bill and Beachbody® changed my life that day.

I wanted to meet the people involved in this amazing company, so I attended as many live events as I could.

I knew *this* was the culture I wanted to be part of—people I felt empowered to surround myself with, from whom I could learn and cultivate the type of mindsets they seemed to embody: imperfect individuals committed to growth, taking control of their agency and autonomy through their actions.

Although I didn't wind up building a successful coaching business, and even though it took me eight more years of breaking up and then giving him "one more chance" before I finally got divorced, my fitness journey became one of the most transformative aspects of my life and a driving force in figuring out how to become the best "me" in all areas of life, including breaking free of codependency.

And that is where I found myself when, in the spring of 2011, I discovered that he had spent all of that money on all of that destruction.

I knew I needed to put a plan into action to propel me in the direction that I was yearning for in my life. Chalene Johnson was instrumental in helping me. I had been working out daily with her programs, building my physical and mental strength.

I had received a few emails from Chalene about an event that she, along with Bo Eason and Roger Love, was going to be speaking at called "World's Greatest Speaker Training" by Brendon Burchard. The more I learned about Brendon and his strategically powerful teaching, the more I wanted to learn more *from* him. He had become part of my morning routine, so I decided to go to this training to learn how to tell my story to inspire other women.

As I was helping run my husband's construction company, I used his bank card and purchased my plane ticket. But he was threatened by my desire to tell my story, so he tried to stop me from going. He drained most of the remaining funds from that account and moved them to another one, to which I had no access. When I attempted to buy my event ticket, I realized what he had done.

I had to take mental stock of my situation, get resourceful, and figure it out! I was not going to let this stop me from moving forward with my life. It was time to let the power of intention kick back in. I reached out to the Burchard group. I knew it was a long shot, but what came of it was the most beautiful display of grace and the very beginning of my journey toward you.

Here are a few short snippets from the email that explained my situation in great detail:

K.I.S.S. CODEPENDENCY GOODBYE: KEEP IT SIMPLE & SCIENTIFIC

From: Eileen Sakofsky
Sent: Monday, May 09, 2011 5:48 PM
To: Jen
Subject: Urgent Request Regarding San Diego Event This Weekend

Hi Jennifer,

Please read the following letter. I would be deeply appreciative if you would forward this to Brendon.

Thank You,
Eileen

> Dear Brendon and Chalene,
>
> After much internal deliberation and frustration, and also encouragement from my friend and upline Beachbody Coach Traci Morrow, I have sat down to write this email several times... and subsequently erased it every time.
>
> However, after reading Brendon's Transformational Truth #2 this morning, which ended with "As you move forward, may the gates to possibility always swing wide open for you," I knew that I HAD to do this.
>
> I am asking for help in opening those gates.
>
> I feel so compelled to be there this weekend that I am reaching out to you to see if you would be willing to let me attend the training. I am not asking for a handout, just a hand up to the new possibilities of my life. I would be willing to help you in any capacity to barter for the admission price or pay you later as I can.
>
> I have an exceptional story to tell, one that I am still going through and working very hard to change. I need to learn how to effectively share my story because I know that it will undoubtedly encourage and help many, many women.

Long before I became a Beachbody Coach, I knew one day I would be a motivational speaker and author. I feel like God has been preparing me for this MY WHOLE LIFE.

So, if you see fit to help me, I also believe you will be helping many others through your caring and generosity.

My friend Traci sent this to me when I asked her for her opinion prior to sending that letter...

From: Traci Morrow
Sent: Mon, May 9, 2011, 12:00 PM
To: Me

SO BEAUTIFULLY WRITTEN!! :) Hit send – I'm praying. <3 <3 <3

I prayed a lot, and could hardly breathe while I was waiting for a response. Here is a bit of it.

Hi Eileen-

Thank you for your transparency and honesty in the message you sent me yesterday.

I love that you've asked us to help you open the gates that Brendon talks about in his Transformation Truths, and I know that he would be honored by your story.

We very rarely make deals or accommodations to allow someone to attend an event without having fully paid. We also hardly ever make exceptions to our policies, as we don't believe it's fair to those who have paid the full ticket price to attend.

That said, I believe your situation is unique, and we'd like to help. We believe in your story, and in your power to make a difference in the lives of women... So c'mon out to California and learn the tools you'll need to be successful.

I was so immensely relieved and full of gratitude and elatedness when I received her response that I just sat and cried.

THE POWER OF INTENTION COMBINED WITH ACTION HAS NO LIMITS

When I got to the event, they told me that they believed in me and were looking forward to seeing the impactful difference I would make with the knowledge that I would gain over the weekend. It has taken me a very long time to get here, but I never gave up! It was a life-changing weekend. I was in awe of the level of highly accomplished individuals that I had just positioned myself to be learning with.

But when I realized that these were very elite professionals with whom I was in attendance, I felt so inadequate. My life was a mess. I was the "codependent," struggling wife of an addict. I didn't even have a job, let alone a massively successful career. However:

- I decided that I belonged there;
- I knew that I was there for a reason;
- I didn't allow myself to feel intimidated.

Instead, I *decided* to just "Be The Best" (as Bo Eason says) by being exactly who I was at that time in my life and to tell my new story of where I was going and who I was resolute on becoming.

And then I returned home to total destruction.

I had received several very heart-wrenching phone calls from my kids during the weekend. They were in second and fourth grade at the time, and their dad had left them alone while he was out drugging. All weekend, I was emotionally torn. I felt immensely guilty being away from them while they were dealing with their dad's insanity, but I was away to learn skills to be able to provide a better life for them and for all of the women and other kids that I believed I would one day impact.

I had gained so much clarity over the weekend training that once I was back home and living in such a toxic environment, I knew we had to leave… again. With the help of my best friend, Dionne—*with whom I've shared a friendship that has gotten us both through the thick and thin of life*—I devised a plan to literally escape once the school year was over. At the beginning of June 2011, we were on a plane headed safely back to San Diego. And just one week later, I drove up to Los Angeles to the Beachbody Coach's Summit! It was the positive culture that I chose to surround myself with and learn from that kept me moving towards a better life. Still, it ultimately took one last try until it ended with a restraining order and divorce in 2016.

In 2017, six full years after attending World's Greatest Speaker Training, I was able to finally attend Bo Eason's Personal Story Power Event in Santa Barbara. It took me six years, but I got there! What I had learned from both Brendon and Bo in 2011 made sparks fly in my soul, as what they were teaching validated my belief in my desire to tell my story. I learned from Bo the magnitude of the power of story: how it is "the connective tissue" that binds us all together, that enables us to transform and enrich each other's lives. We connect bits of ourselves in someone else's story that resonates within our own so that we can grow.

> *"A personal story creates connective tissue that allows people to connect with you, understand you, and follow you."*
>
> *"When you tell your story, your audience is watching and looking to hear what your story is, so they can locate themselves inside of your story. People are looking to find themselves inside of your story."*
>
> *"A personal story creates connection and intimacy. Personal equals universal."*
>
> –Bo Eason

I was beyond excited to go to this event! But a week before the event, my now ex-husband wrapped his truck (that he was living in) around a tree in the middle of the night. Many hours later, he texted me a picture of his smashed, blood-drenched face. I knew he was in serious trouble. I picked him up and took him to the emergency room. They told me that he would have died in just a few more hours if I hadn't brought him there. They released him two days before I was to leave for my event. He was supposed to go to a homeless convalescent place, but he bailed out because he was afraid of getting arrested. He was now wandering, dazed and confused, on the streets and calling me for help. He didn't want me to go. I almost didn't go to the event, but I knew that no matter what, I had to go.

He got himself in this situation by driving high in the middle of the night and hitting a tree. I made the decision to take care of *me*. I got on that plane and headed to Santa Barbara. It was an extraordinary training. The welcome banner outside said it all: "Destroy Everything That Is Not Excellent."

Post-divorce, I encountered different but still extraordinarily challenging, emotionally exhausting situations, battles, and obstacles in my determination to create a better life, one of which was starting my own construction company, which failed after the first job. But out of it came more clarity, strength, and growth. I learned that I truly am in control of not being controlled or manipulated and not allowing emotional abuse back into my life *for any reason, even with A LOT of money involved*. It ended with me suing the general contractor... and winning in mediation. It was truly a David vs. Goliath victory, and it made me realize that it was not really what I wanted to do. I was watching motivational videos to keep my head focused in the right direction while figuring out what to do next when a random video popped up. I didn't know who Tom Bilyeu was, but the title caught my eye: "Who Are You Prepared To Become?" That question was pivotal for me because I had just lost my business. I wasn't sure what my next *move* was, but I knew *who* I was prepared to become. His message was riveting and was all about acquiring the skills you need to accomplish the goals you desire. You should go watch it.

> "Once you understand that **that's** what you have to do to get control of yourself... You have to stay focused on something. You have to learn the discipline and apply it to your path to success. And that's the fucking secret. There really is no grand mystery. And that... is the best possible news I could give you. Because it doesn't matter what you're born with. It doesn't even matter who you are. What matters is who you want to

become and the price that you're willing to pay to get there. Let me tell you this. The price is known. And that price is the acquisition of skills."

–Tom Bilyeu

I can't emphasize that enough as being an absolute foundational point of clarification to make, and to keep making, with yourself.

Who are you prepared to become? Who do you want to be? It is absolutely 100 percent *in your control* to acquire and master the skills to be successful in overcoming the MINDSETS of CODEPENDENCY that hold you back in all areas of your life.

Discovering Tom opened up a whole new level of learning. He talks a lot about human potential:

"Humans are the ultimate adaptation machine, but so many people focus on all of their limitations rather than their potential. Because of that misplaced focus, they end up proving that their limitations are real. Simply shifting your focus to just how much humans are capable of, on the other hand, causes action, because the cause-and-effect relationship between effort and progress becomes obvious."

"The most exciting thing that I've ever realized about being a human is that what the brain is designed to do allows us to change. So make no mistake, right now, what you're choosing to focus on, it matters. It will determine the course of your life, and that the very course of your life is determined by nobody but you. **It is not determined by people who have victimized you. It is not determined by anything that has happened in your past.** *It is determined right here, right now, in this moment, by what you choose to focus your energies on."*

–Tom Bilyeu

All of *that* resonated deeply with me.

On his show *Impact Theory,* Tom engaged in growth-oriented, empowering conversations with the highest achievers, most of whom started out at the most humble and challenging beginnings.

Their struggles became their superpowers. I learned from so many of them, and a few in particular—Lewis Howes, Ed Mylett, and Dr. Andrew Huberman—have deeply impacted me.

Lewis Howes had suffered sexual abuse as a child, a career-ending football injury as an adult and was broke, lost, and living on his sister's couch. Yet he found his way beyond all of that to become the Lewis Howes that we all know and love today. I tell you that to encourage you that, although his circumstances may be completely different from yours, you can also find a path beyond whatever you may be going through.

I was in my own state of challenging circumstances after losing my construction company but trying so hard to figure out how to change it. I was so emboldened by Lewis's story that I enrolled in his online course about how to self-publish a book. I sat and wrote for three months straight. Lewis gave me the belief that I could actually write a book, which *finally* started my authorship journey, and his amazing community gave me the encouragement to get it done. Although that first book was nowhere near ready to be published (which I briefly did), getting it in the mail was tangible evidence of my efforts, and I was really proud of myself for taking the actions to do it. I am deeply grateful to Lewis and his community.

I had listened to many powerful, inspiring conversations on Impact Theory, but I didn't feel a personal connection with any of their stories in the way that I did with Ed Mylett's. Obviously our journeys have been extremely different, but the essence of what his origin story was and how it turned into his message and mission, as well as just some of the *things* that he has done—both deeply inspired me and, at the same time, made me laugh out loud at some of the hilarious similarities. I felt an almost kindred connection that I was immediately drawn to, and throughout their conversation I had a couple of profound "aha" full-circle moments of familiarity.

Ed truly exemplifies what it means to not let your past define your future. Instead, he turned some of his greatest pain into his most powerful and impactful qualities. In very different ways, both of our lives were shaped by loving someone with addiction. His father was an alcoholic when Ed was a little boy (who thankfully found sobriety by the time Ed was a teen). Ed's life mission became helping people reach their highest potential—and teaching how your *personal identity* is the driving force behind that transformation.

"Identity is the governor of our lives. It's the invisible force that no one understands, and once they do understand and get hold of it, their life can change."

–Ed Mylett

The first full-circle "aha" moment came when I heard Tom Bilyeu mention that he'd first heard that idea about identity being the driver of your life from Tony Robbins—because Tony had been a formative voice in my own life since I was a teenager. And realizing that both Tom and Ed had also been inspired by Tony as they were learning on their own journeys just made me feel like I belonged there learning from them. If you're fortunate enough to find teachers who leave a positive imprint on your life, whose words stick, it can help you shape your self-belief—and your life.

And then I literally had to laugh out loud. Some of the things Ed did when he was still totally broke but finding his way to success were just so... *me*. He was definitely a bit more audacious, as he once Velcroed his car to look like a Mercedes, which I never did *that, but* things like it—scrappy, strategic, and driven by a relentless vision to make life feel like I wanted it to be for me and my kids, even while living in motels.

And just the crazy similarities: His wife's car got repossessed—been there. He showered at the pool when their water was shut off—I showered at a beach park (which, by the way, is where I discovered the amazing power of cold showers). I had lived in Cocolalla and Sandpoint, Idaho — and he and his family had lived in Coeur d'Alene. And our birthdays are even a day apart! But beyond the fun facts, we share something deeper: a relentless hunger for a better life.

But what struck me most in my second full-circle moment was when Tom asked Ed how he built self-confidence before he had the results to "prove" himself and had a message worth sharing even before his life reflected the success of it—because that's exactly what I wrote to Brendon Burchard in 2011. I had no platform, no money, and a life still in chaos—but I knew I had a story that could change other women's lives, and I was determined to learn how to tell it.

At the end of that interview, Tom asked Ed what kind of impact he wanted to leave on the world. He said, "I want to inspire as many people as

I physically can... to chase down the ultimate version of them in their way, in their place, and in their space." Like Ed, I have always believed that your past doesn't disqualify you—it *prepares* you. And in fact, it's often the very thing that most qualifies you. As I once heard him say, which took my breath away, "*If you don't believe you're qualified, if you don't believe you can do it, you're gonna miss those moments in your life, and your entire existence here wasn't what it was supposed to be.*"

To me, that's the whole point of learning from someone who's already done what you hope to do: so that *you* can turn around and pass that wisdom on. That's the message I want to pass on to you: *you* matter. Your voice, your truth, your scars—they matter. Find your voice. Be bold. Let your experiences be your gas pedal, not your brakes.

I have been learning from Ed since that episode in 2018. Out of all the amazing mentors who have impacted my journey, his voice resonates the deepest when I start doubting my own ability and allow the fear of the *bigness* of what I am about to do and the dramatic shift in how my own life will transform to dominate my mind. So, through my own determination and his reaffirming wisdom echoing in my head, I keep moving forward towards it.

As I've seen myself evolve from the identity of codependent wife of an addict to ex-wife to struggling single mom to becoming the "me" I always believed I could be, I continue to be inspired by him to keep growing into the elevated version of myself that's ready to present her voice to the world. Because it matters. It has a ripple effect. And just like Ed—maybe, in my own way—I can help change a few people's lives... or perhaps many millions.

The founders of Al-Anon didn't have degrees in psychology, nor were they licensed therapists.

The only thing that "qualified" them to start that program was simply *their* lived experiences as the struggling wives of alcoholics and the desire to help others in their own journey, which they have done worldwide.

The 12-step system, while transformative for many, became the blueprint for how we think about codependency and remains the most widely recognized method for helping people to overcome it, not necessarily because it's the most effective model—but because it was the *first widely accepted* one. As the dominant treatment model of the time, and having shaped decades of *social context and the collective belief system about it,* it is assumed to be the most authoritative. In the absence of alternatives, it became culturally entrenched.

However, as I have discovered, it's staggering to comprehend the amount of information that we now have in the world we now live in and the vast amount of data and understanding of the function of the brain and nervous system that just wasn't available back then.

Women land at a meeting like this because they are desperately seeking a solution. Because of the social context around this program, and in their desperation for things to change in their lives, they follow what the system is directing them to do.

In this way, the 12-step mindset has become more than a program—it's a lens through which millions have learned to see themselves. But what if there's another lens? One that isn't about surrendering your power—but reclaiming it? When we shift the mindset, we shift the outcome.

And science backs that up.

Just ask yourself which you believe has more potential for long-term efficacy.

- Believing that you are inherently defective and need to spend your life asking for those defects to be removed, which if you are still asking, you are still believing.
- Or, believing in the data that proves that you are installed with the most powerful ability to reprogram maladaptive beliefs about yourself to become a better self-identified version of yourself.

As I have learned from Dr. Alia Crum, a tenured professor of psychology at Stanford University and the founder and director of the Stanford Mind and Body Lab (whom I discovered through Dr. Andrew Huberman) whose groundbreaking research shows that mindsets—our core beliefs about ourselves and the world—not only influence our motivation but also our biology and behavior.

> *"We define mindsets as core beliefs or assumptions that we have about a domain or category of things that orient us to a particular set of expectations, explanations, and goals."*
>
> *"Those mindsets, those core beliefs, orient our thinking, they change what **we expect** will happen to us."*
>
> –Dr. Alia Crum

We all know that mindsets matter; however, Dr. Crum's research provides data on how deeply the effects of mindsets can define us.

That means if we adopt a mindset believing that we have a defect of character, those beliefs can *literally shape our outcomes*. Not because they're objectively true, but because we believe they are. That is the power of social context: it makes certain narratives feel like truth when they may just be tradition.

It is time to introduce a paradigm shift into the zeitgeist—a new, science-based approach rooted in neuroscience, neuroplasticity, and self-directed empowerment... And because *my* entire life's experiences have brought *me* to this understanding, I am uniquely "qualified" to bring this knowledge into it.

That brings me full circle to how I came upon learning about the study of neuroscience and Dr. Andrew Huberman.

SAY OH HELLO, COVID-19

I had been a Lyft driver for about a year and had a steady clientele of business commuters. Just six months earlier, I had finally accomplished moving us into a beautiful big house, and I was able to buy two new cars! But then, in the blink of an eye, my business literally dissolved into nonexistence. I was seriously panicked at first, but because of all the peaks and valleys that I have experienced, I knew that falling apart wasn't the answer and that I needed to figure out a way to pivot. I started to deliver Uber Eats because everyone was at home ordering food. Now, instead of engaging in conversation all day, I was alone in my car, so I turned it into my drive-time university! Who knew that delivering food would become a major transformation point in my life! As usual, I was looking for something to listen to that I could learn from and be inspired by. I just happened to see this thumbnail for Tom's interview with Dr. Andrew Huberman: "Growth Mindset Biohacks." That sounded interesting!

I was completely blown away by what I heard. It felt like he was explaining my life's story... *scientifically.* Learning how the brain and nervous system work helped me make sense of *why* the efforts that I have made and the focused actions that I have taken were effective. I knew that I had just discovered the science to articulate strategies for breaking free of codependency and making lifelong change!

It was the information that I never knew I had always been looking for.

And *this* was where my journey was supposed to lead me all along!

"What I would love everyone to know about the brain is that it has this adaptive feature, this ability to generate self-directed, adaptive plasticity. I think that when one accepts that as a hardwired feature of the way they're built, it can potentially be a game-changer. That this collection of cells in your skull was designed to be customized to your liking is really, truly a possibility.

You can really harness these mechanisms. And they're really quite simple.

My hope is that people would know that they have this capacity. And then of course, my additional wish would be that they would leverage that capacity."

"So if we focus on tools that reflect the activity of neural circuits that are present in an animal and in humans, there's a beauty in that logic because we can just say, you know...

Nature, God, The Universe... whatever your beliefs or structure is, doesn't really matter.

> *There's an elegance to placing these neurons, and these hormones, and these organs in all species. It says they were really designed for that purpose."*
>
> –Dr. Andrew Huberman

And there it was... I *finally* found it. The positive, universal, simple solution that I was seeking!

My goal is not to diminish anyone's belief in God; quite the contrary. If you truly believe that God created you, then I would posit that perhaps instead of praying for *defects to be removed from you*, you might pray for a deeper understanding of how to better utilize the powerful *systems* that He installed *in you*.

I have since listened to hundreds of hours of Dr. Huberman—*Andrew*—on various podcasts, as well as in-depth conversations with other neuroscientists, psychologists, and the like on his own podcast called *The Huberman Lab*. One such discussion was with Dr. Anna Lembke, who is a psychiatrist and the chief of the Stanford Addiction Medicine Dual Diagnosis Clinic at Stanford University. She is a specialist in the opioid epidemic in the United States and the author of *Drug Dealer, MD: How Doctors Were Duped, Patients Got Hooked, and Why It's So Hard to Stop*, as well as *Dopamine Nation*. They were discussing the notion of addicts getting addicted to AA.

> **Andrew:** There seems to be a circuit in the brain of addicts to discuss and want to kind of talk about their recovery a lot. And I mention this not to poke at them, but rather the opposite, because I think that one thing that is challenging, at least for me, is having friends that have a propensity for drug or alcohol addiction—not all of them, but certainly some of them. When they're talking about their recovery, I feel like it's all they talk about. This meeting, that meeting, that meeting. So what I'm really asking here is, can we become addicted to sobriety? Can the meetings themselves become their own form of a dopamine hit? And again, I'm not being disparaging; I just want to understand this.

Dr Lembke: Right, so yes, so a lot of times patients will say to me, "Oh, you know, I don't want to go to AA. It's a cult. And my response to that is because it's a cult, which is exactly why it works. Because yes, it is much better for you to be addicted to AA and to recovery than *almost* any other addiction I could think of.

When I heard this discussion, it was a validation of my assessment and feelings about the 12-step meeting that I had attended, which felt programmed and cultish... *because it is the same exact system.*

I totally agree with Dr. Lembke on the notion that an addict is better off being "addicted" to AA than to crack, meth, alcohol, or any other substance of abuse. I absolutely would rather have had my husband be addicted to meetings than to all of the drugs that he was.

And I believe one of the "almosts" in her sentence is codependency:

- You are really only addicted to your own limiting beliefs, not to the addict;
- Codependency becomes part of your personal identity;
- It becomes a neurochemical feedback loop that keeps you subconsciously believing that there is something inherently defective in you, as Step 7 in particular is supposed to be a lifetime commitment of asking for the removal of character defects. Again, the more you ask, the more you believe there is reason to;
- It is a cyclical scenario, which is why you may make progress through this program but feel the need to stay attached to the *system*, in essence, being "codependent" on the program, which becomes part of your story and part of your identity.

And that *identity* holds a powerful grip.

That's when I came to the obvious conclusion of an unintentional consequence:

> **The 12-step system keeps you neurochemically connected to your *identity* as a codependent.**

"When you believe something, there are chemical reward systems in your mind that are associated with just repeating that belief."

"So the more I see stuff that verifies what I already think or feel, the more dopamine and adrenaline are released into my system."

–Dr. Andrew Huberman

Staying indoctrinated in the same thought processes, with the same type of people, while continually asking to be freed of an inherent defectiveness that a system presupposes of you; in essence programming that belief into you, for years of your life, all in an effort to try to find your freedom from it *Just Doesn't Make Sense.* **There is no true freedom in that.**

So, what is the solution? There is a better way! It's an inside job... an *intrinsic reward* job!

Do hard shit, show up for yourself, and mentally reward yourself for it!

It's about more empowering programming.

After many years of finding my own way forward and learning what I have about the way our nervous system, our reward system, and the wiring of our neural circuits in the brain work, I came to realize that *that* is the key to overcoming codependency. The fact is, you were designed to have agency over your own machinery. Science proves that you have the ability to hardwire better programming for more adaptive connections that create a healthier mind. It simply comes down to learning how to have better leverage of your autonomic nervous system and learning a few basic things about it.

- Self-directed adaptive plasticity
- Self-generated optic flow
- Self-induced stress inoculation
- Interoception/exteroception
- Intrinsic/extrinsic rewards (the dopamine reward system)
- Top-down processing... and more fun things!

*"I think that teaching autonomic control to kids and to adults, whether they have trauma or not, I think, is a fundamental skill that's more important, in my opinion, than almost any other skill, just like walking and talking. If you can learn to control your autonomic nervous system, a whole world of possibilities opens up to you. It's because autonomic control ultimately is control over our behavior. And so learning autonomic control, I feel like that is **the** issue for mental health."*

–Dr. Andrew Huberman

That may sound complicated, but you will be happy to hear that, just as Andrew said, it really is quite simple. And when I heard him say that, my lightbulb went on, and I thought... *They're ALL overcomplicating this.* The saying "Keep it simple, stupid" came to mind, which morphed into "Keep it simple, sister," as we are *not* stupid, which then became "Keep It Simple and Scientific."

BAM! The **K.I.S.S. SYSTEM™**—A Non-12-Step, Neuroscientific Data-Driven Solution—was born. It's time to **K.I.S.S. Codependency Goodbye** with powerful, science-backed tools that put *you* back in the driver's seat. But this isn't just a method—it's a movement. Because it's time to **kick codependency to the curb** and say **hellooo ME** to the bold, badass, confident woman you were always meant to be.

Welcome to **#HelloMeMovement—The Revolution**: a fierce uprising of women reclaiming their power, rewriting their programming, and rising into the truth of who they are. We're Upgrading. Rewiring. Rising.

The **K.I.S.S. SYSTEM™** is the method.

#HelloMeMovement is the mission.

#HelloMeMovement—The Revolution: *Coming Soon.*

Is your mind uploaded with self-defeating thoughts of unworthiness, unimportance, neediness, control issues, insecurity, lack, failure, and/or just not being good enough?

Do you find yourself repeating patterns that you know are not working? Have you poured your mental, emotional, intellectual, physical, spiritual, sexual, creative, financial, and/or time resources into others as a means to feel valued and validated? Have you neglected to pursue your own life and dreams to the fullest of your capabilities?

Instead of finding fulfillment, have you become more depleted and frustrated... feeling used and abused? Does your voice feel diminished—do you feel like a victim?

Do you ever ask yourself, *What the hell is wrong with me?*

Your mind is operating within a vicious feedback loop cycle of hard-wired programming.

But did you know that you actually have full control of all of these beliefs and perceptions?

The process of changing your life from that of miserably codependent to happy and free doesn't need to be complicated. You just have to be willing to let go of what (and who) is not working and be intentional and determined in learning *and doing* what will. The good news is that the adult brain *can change,* and that once you learn how, you become the one in control of the programming!

The K.I.S.S. SYSTEM™ implements powerful, data-driven, science-based solutions within a framework of simple strategies I call the *Sexy Six. Why Sexy Six?* Because confidence is sexy. Reclaiming your life should feel exciting, empowering—and yes, sexy within and for *yourself*, with a bit of cheeky fun and sass, because having levity in life is an important aspect of being healthy! You've been through enough. Let's make the rest of this reclamation journey something you *want* to do. Chef's K.I.S.S. to the *Sexy Six!*

1. **VISION: The Seduction of Seeing Possibility & Visual Vibe Shift** Vision is the first spark—the irresistible pull toward what's possible when you let yourself dream unapologetically big and create a crystal-clear vision of who you want to be and what you see for your future—but this isn't *just* about dreaming big and seeing possibility. It's about how your *actual visual system* affects your nervous system and state of mind. Learn to use your eyes—yes, your eyes—to calm your body, gain clarity, and create mental space for transformation. Think of it as turning your walk into a *Walkitation*™—a movement-based meditation that rewires your stress response through self-generated optic flow. You were made to move, so move baby, move!

You will learn to stop living within a myopic view of your life and to expand the sight line of possibility of who you are capable of being.

2. PERCEPTION: The Mindset Makeover

This is where the magic happens. You don't just change your mind—you change how you see the world. Reframing isn't surface-level. It's a neuroscience-backed superpower. Perception is your brain's interpretation of reality—and it's editable. You'll learn how to update your lens so that fear, shame, and outdated beliefs no longer color your world. You don't have to keep reacting from old code. Let's rewrite it.

3. BELIEF: Confidence Couture

Slip into the version of you that believes she can. Because belief isn't born—it's built, styled, and worn like your fiercest outfit: with intention, repetition, and a little attitude. Your beliefs are not facts—but they do shape your identity. In this step, we dismantle the false narratives you've inherited or absorbed and replace them with truths rooted in neuroscience and self-compassion. You'll begin to embody the identity of a woman who is worthy, capable, and completely whole.

4. INTENTION: *Desire on Purpose*

This is your why—big and bodacious. You're not just hoping life gets better. You're choosing it, designing it, and showing up for it. This is where clarity meets chemistry. When your intentions are emotionally compelling and aligned with your values, they activate your brain's reward system. Intentions aren't vague wishes. When grounded in meaning, they activate your prefrontal cortex and your dopamine reward circuitry—making purposeful action more accessible and repeatable. We'll align your intentions with who you are becoming, so they pull you forward instead of weighing you down. That means more dopamine, more motivation, and a higher likelihood you'll follow through.

5. ACTION: *Lit by Dopamine, Led by Desire*
The Sexy Science of Getting Sh*t Done:
Desire, Drive, and Doing the Damn Thing
We don't "Fake It Till You Make It."
We "Take Action Until You Achieve It!"

You've imagined it—now you move like it. Strategic. Bold. Repeatable.

Your actions are no longer random—they're patterns of becoming. And one of the most powerful actions you'll take is movement. Because physical fitness isn't just about changing your body—it's about changing your brain. You'll be taking all kinds of new, realigned actions—and one of the most transformative will be learning to move with purpose because nothing regulates your nervous system like movement. When you engage your body, you're not just snatching your waist—you're creating **self-generated optic flow, self-induced stress inoculation,** and **top-down control.**

That's why I call it **Fitness for Your Lifetime—Not Just Your Waistline.**™ Because this isn't about flat abs; it's about full autonomy. Every time you follow through, your brain registers it as proof that change is possible—and rewarding. Tiny actions create powerful neural feedback loops. The more you move, the more aligned and empowered you feel. You'll stop the feedback loop of being reactionary—and become intentionally **Me-Actionary.** Welcome to behavior change that actually sticks.

6. ACKNOWLEDGEMENT: The Celebration Circuit—Celebrate The Sexy New You!
Celebrate your rewiring. Reinforce new pathways with self-sourced reward chemistry. Because the woman becoming her next best self deserves recognition. When you acknowledge your own growth, you literally rewire your brain to seek more of it. Gratitude, recognition, and celebration aren't woo—they're strategy. Let's teach your nervous system that thriving is your new normal. Acknowledgment

isn't optional—it's brain fuel. Noticing and celebrating your growth creates a self-reinforcing cycle of motivation and progress. It wires your brain to expect success and appreciate effort, making forward movement feel natural, not forced.

Your brain wants a win—give it one often!

Within this framework, you'll easily learn how to regulate your physiology, rewire your thought patterns, and reclaim your personal identity, self-worth, and—most importantly—your *autonomy*. You'll learn to live free of the outdated, toxic narratives around "codependency" that have distracted you from the fulfilling life you deserve. Let's get you reconnected to *you*.

It's important to note that many professionals have estimated an alarming number of people have identified themselves as being "codependent." According to Mental Health America, codependency affects approximately 20-25 percent of the population.[1] According to the NIH, 40 million Americans, primarily women, have been labeled as codependent.[2] However, some estimates suggest that over 90 percent of Americans demonstrate some level of codependent behavior during their lifetimes. *90 percent!!!* And while that is just an estimate, there is a high probability of accuracy, as the term "codependency" has morphed over the years to also encompass a whole bastion of people beyond those in a relationship with an addict but who also struggle with: the need for external validation, lack of self-identity, boundaries, people pleasing, self-confidence, control and the like. It is so culturally embedded into the collective belief structure and mindset of society that it's common to hear people blithely say "I'm *so* codependent." Just remember that beliefs become behaviors, and behaviors become beliefs.

It's a feedback loop.

So with such a high percentage of people identifying themselves this way, I would say that that could be considered a crisis; however, I believe it

---

1. "Co-Dependency." Mental Health America, December 3, 2024. https://mhanational.org/resources/co-dependency/.
2. RA;, Hughes-Hammer C; Martsolf DS; Zeller. "Depression and Codependency in Women." Archives of psychiatric nursing. Accessed July 23, 2025. https://pubmed.ncbi.nlm.nih.gov/9868824/.

is not a crisis of codependency but more that it is an autonomic control, human condition crisis.

So, in conclusion, when you are living in entrenched thinking with a myopic view of your life, it is so easy to overcomplicate your path to living a healthy, fulfilled future. My hope is that I may have inspired you to broaden your view and have given you a new outlook with simple strategies and tools to get you there. Once you start taking back control, you will be amazed at the places you may see yourself go in your life.

Who would ever have thought that the journey of a once-homeless girl determined to figure out how to overcome the devastating so-called codependent life that she had been living would lead her to learning about and leveraging the knowledge of *neuroscience*?

Not me.

But that is the beautiful thing about your amazing, powerful brain. As Dr. Andrew Huberman said, *"It was designed to be customized to your liking."* Once you start understanding that you have the ability to take control of its programming and that it has the capacity to make hardwired change, you literally never know the places it can take you and what extraordinary things that you are capable of accomplishing... *no matter how bad it was where you started.*

I believe that because I had an intentional determination to change and a crystal-clear vision of where I wanted this road to take me, many incredible teachers have appeared in my path who have helped to show me the way. I am continually being stretched to learn more as I journey forward. As each mentor came with their own unique life experiences and insights, they have each had their own unique impact on my life, just as I am endeavoring to do for you. Everything you've experienced in your life has brought you to this point, and though you may not be where you want to be, you're just not there *yet*. Keep going.

Over time, I came to realize something remarkable: *all* of my mentors know each other—but they don't all know me... at least, *not yet*. Still, the ripple effect they've had on my life is undeniable. My intention and hope are that this is where that ripple reaches you.

And my closing thought: If there is one resounding connective message thread between them all, it is this—What I needed, I already had. That if I truly wanted to change, the ability to do it was already within me. I just had to cultivate it and utilize it. What is that, you might ask?

Well, quite simply... *me* and my amazing, powerful nervous system and brain.

And the good news is... you have one too!

Eileen Sakofsky is a writer, speaker, and resilience renegade who *fiercely* believes that your circumstances are *not* outcome-determinative. At one point during her thirty-year battle with her ex-husband's addictions—which took her down a long road of codependency and abuse, eventually leading to her being homeless with kids, having to live with family and friends, and in and out of hotels and motels for many years—she strategically rented a room in an extended-stay motel located within one of Denver's wealthiest neighborhoods, just so her kids could enroll in top-tier elementary and middle schools that would eventually feed into one of the most prestigious and academically rigorous public high schools in Colorado. And that bold move paid off. Her daughter became a confident, intelligent, achievement-driven powerhouse full of laughter, light, compassion, and determination who, just four seasons into the sport, had a meteoric rise and earned a spot on a Worlds-Level All-Star Competitive Cheerleading Team, performing at the highest level in the sport, and who has carried those qualities into the pursuits of her life.

Her son is a passionate learner, kind-hearted, richly engaging conversationalist, and multi-instrumental musician who has a deep love of a broad and diverse range of music. He is a deep-thinking academic pursuing his dreams with undeterred perseverance, majoring in math with a double minor in physics and music. Eileen's proudest success is knowing that she also instilled that belief in her kids, witnessing in awe what they have chosen to make of themselves and the paths that they have chosen for their lives, despite what their childhood circumstances had been.

In her journey to thrive beyond that relationship, Eileen rebuilt her life from the ground up—literally. She is the creator of The K.I.S.S SYSTEM™: *Keep It Simple & Scientific*, a neuroscience-based, non-12-step path to freedom from codependency. Her upcoming book series includes *Dear*

Codependency, You Can KISS My BRAIN Goodbye: I've Changed My MIND About You—a look at how profoundly the patterns of your mind and your mindsets affect your life, and the magnitude of the power you possess to change them... *Not him, Code Dependent: It's Not Your Codependency, It's Your Neurochemistry*—a bold reframe that empowers women through science, self-compassion, and the brain's power to rewire for lasting change, and SELF*ish* A.F.—a data-driven deep dive into becoming your most powerfully authentic self. With a mix of heart, humor, and hard-won wisdom, Eileen helps women reclaim their identity, retrain their brain, and write a better next chapter.

∼

To connect with Eileen:

LinkedIn: https://www.linkedin.com/in/eileensakofsky?utm_source=share&utm_campaign=share_via&utm_content=profile&utm_medium=android_app

—

Instagram: @eileensakofsky

—

Facebook: https://www.facebook.com/eileen.sakofsky?mibextid=kFxxJD

—

EileenSakofsky.com

GRACEFULLY UNBREAKABLE
BY EMILY KAMATA

THE FALL

"I regret to tell you... This will be your last day."

The words hit before I had even taken a seat. For a second, I thought I had misheard.

Across from me stood my manager, who had flown in from Los Gatos, near San Francisco. She wasn't supposed to be in Japan. Not today, and certainly not without warning.

Days earlier, we had exchanged friendly emails. So when I stepped forward to greet her, stunned to see her there, I instinctively went in for a hug. But her body was stiff, her smile forced.

That was the moment I knew something was wrong.

As she continued speaking, the room began to whirl around me. My heart was pounding, my breath shallow.

Then it hit me—I was being fired.

Just that morning, I had been at my desk, working as the Japanese language specialist on Netflix's localization team.

I was one of the few bilingual professionals entrusted to bridge the Tokyo office and Los Gatos headquarters as the platform ramped up its expansion into Japan in 2015. It was a high-pressure role, but an exciting one that came with a $120k salary. This job felt like everything I had worked for. I thrived in the challenge, energized by the fast-paced environment and the chance to be a part of something global.

I thought I was doing well, but tension had been growing between me and the marketing director in Japan. My job required me to build a strong relationship with him, as he was essentially running the business locally. I had gone out of my way to be accommodating, even translating fifty-page storylines overnight (this was before AI or any sort of machine translation). But no matter how hard I tried, it never felt like enough. I couldn't shake the feeling that he simply didn't like me.

Now, I was being let go just five months after starting the job—suddenly, without warning, without any conversation. My manager told me I had failed to meet the expectations of both the headquarters and the Japan office.

My cheeks flushed, suddenly hot. I could feel the tears building before I could stop them. I tried to speak, tried to defend myself, but the words came out cracked and broken. "This isn't fair," I said, my voice shaking. But there was no response—just a quiet, procedural stillness.

Then the HR director walked in. She read off the severance terms. My laptop was removed. I wasn't even allowed to return to my desk. Someone else was sent to pack up my things.

I sat there, still stunned. The office was brand new, and the smell of fresh upholstery still lingered in the air. I stared at the yellow and blue accents in the furniture and thought to myself, "It was too good to be true."

That morning, I had walked into the building with a title, a $120k salary, and the trust of a global brand. I walked out with none of it.

And what hurt most wasn't just the job. It was the silence from my manager, the woman I had trusted as a mentor. She escorted me to the elevator, said almost nothing, and avoided eye contact. Whatever warmth we had shared before was gone.

As the doors closed behind me, I felt like my entire life had collapsed. What I didn't realize at that time was that this wasn't the end. It was the beginning of something entirely different.

BETWEEN TWO WORLDS

Let me take you back for a moment to help you understand who I am and how I ended up in that elevator.

I've spent my entire life living between different languages and cultures.

I was born in 1979 as the only daughter of a strict Taiwanese father and a gentle Japanese mother. My father had built a business selling biotechnology products for agriculture. We weren't super rich, but we were comfortable. We traveled the world for family vacations, and they were able to send me to an international school in Tokyo, which was an English-speaking Catholic school with students from over fifty different countries.

In class, I was encouraged to speak up, ask questions, challenge norms, and think critically. It was a deeply Western education, and I embraced it. I learned to express my opinions in fluent English, think globally, and dream big.

But at home, where we spoke Japanese, those skills had no place. My mother would remind me, "Don't challenge your father. Just obey." And so, I obeyed.

I learned early on that I had to switch modes instantly. I could debate in class, then return home and fall silent at the dinner table. I was afraid to ask my parents for help with my homework, not because they didn't care, but because I didn't want to embarrass them for not understanding English.

Outside, I was the perfect straight-A student. Inside, I was quietly unraveling. I played the role of being put together while never truly feeling whole.

That fracture followed me into adulthood. I became a professional conference interpreter out of necessity—to keep my two broken halves intact and to earn a living through my ability to speak two languages. But even then, I didn't feel like my identity made sense or could provide any real value in this world.

So, when I landed the job at Netflix, it finally felt like the pieces were coming together. For the first time, my bilingual, bicultural background was being recognized as a business asset—something valuable and needed for the company to successfully localize its platform in Japan.

And then, in a matter of minutes, it was all stripped away. Once again, I was the woman who couldn't make sense of her identity or value.

This story is for the woman who feels the same.

The one who lives between identities.

The one who doesn't fit neatly into a box but still dreams of building something of her own.

The woman who wants to make an impact without shouting for attention.

The one who doubts if she's "too quiet" to lead.

I didn't build my business by becoming louder. I didn't succeed by chasing attention. I built it by embracing the very things that made me different. I built it by becoming something else entirely:

Gracefully Unbreakable.

And what happened next, just after I stepped out of that elevator, was where everything really began.

Back to the elevator.

The elevator hit the ground floor. I stepped into the lobby, then out onto the street. The heat was already rising—one of those early summer days when the pavement starts to warm up and everything smells like concrete and sunlight. People moved around me, going about their day, but I felt like I was walking through fog. My head was throbbing.

Somewhere between the shock and the sunlight, I knew what I needed to do next.

ERASING MY NAME

Out on the sidewalk, I took out my phone and called the CEO of the translation firm I had just signed on at Netflix. His company had secured a major contract, and I didn't want him blindsided. He picked up quickly, cheerful as usual, and I kept my voice steady.

"I wanted to let you know," I said, "I've been let go from Netflix. This has nothing to do with you or your firm. I'll make sure the transition goes smoothly."

He paused, clearly surprised but grateful. We hung up shortly after.

I put my phone away and kept walking. I barely remember the rest of the route home. I was moving, but nothing felt real. When I got back to my apartment, I sat down in the dark. No lights. No TV. Just silence.

That was the first time reality hit me. I had no job, no plan, and—single and unmarried—no safety net.

A few days later, the same CEO I had called reached out to me. He said he wanted to help and offered me freelance work. It was extremely generous of him, and this was a lifeline thrown to me while I was drowning. But we had one thing to navigate.

He wanted to avoid any potential issues with Netflix if he gave me freelance work translating their content. He didn't think there would be any backlash, but he didn't want to take the risk. So we agreed for me to use a different name.

I said yes because I needed the work. But something in me sank hard in my stomach.

Just days earlier, I had hired him. I was the decision maker, the one with authority. Now I was taking work from him, and to do so, I had to change my name.

That's what no one tells you about starting over. Sometimes it means becoming someone else just to stay afloat. And now I had a new name and a hidden identity.

And for the first time in my life, I felt truly invisible.

THE QUIET REBUILD AS A FREELANCER

Over the next year, I worked in the shadows under a different name, taking on whatever freelance translation jobs came my way. It wasn't glamorous. It wasn't visible. But I showed up anyway.

Every day, I delivered. Articles, scripts, content guidelines, fandom blogs, e-commerce product descriptions, academic journals—you name it. There was no spotlight, no recognition, no public record of what I was doing. But each project made me sharper and stronger.

Clients started returning because they liked my work. New inquiries trickled in, not from job boards, but through direct messages on LinkedIn. A few came through referrals. Some were friends of former Netflix colleagues who recommended me for Japanese-English translation projects. Those small gestures taught me the importance of staying connected and treating everyone with integrity. Because when you do good work and you treat people with respect, it finds its way back to you, sometimes when you least expect it.

Still, it wasn't easy.

There were days I missed the mark. Clients who weren't satisfied. Moments when I doubted myself. I'd often cry alone at home. Wondering if I was still the same woman who walked out of Netflix. Wondering if I'd ever stop feeling like a failure.

But through the mess, I kept showing up. And little by little, I began to build a reputation with the clients who believed in me as someone they could trust.

As that trust grew, I stopped waiting for people to set the terms. I started proposing solutions. When someone asked for a discount, I didn't shrink; I offered alternatives instead. Quick turnaround times, streamlined processes, and working one-on-one with the reviewers to move projects forward more efficiently.

For the first time, I caught a glimpse of what it meant to do business on my own terms as a professional. There was no corporate brand behind me. No boss telling me what to do, just me and my skills.

And when I felt strong enough, I went back to the work I had loved from the beginning: conference interpretation, which is the art of live, spoken translation.

I opened my calendar to past contacts and referrals. Assignments started to come in. And the confidence I had rebuilt as a freelance translator began to show up in those meetings. In my presence, my pace, and in the way I could move in alignment with the leader in the room quietly, just by how I listened and responded, all while delivering the highest quality of interpretation possible.

I was no longer the woman who had been fired. I was gaining control over my life. And the strength inside of me was like a bright, red-hot fire that emerged from the ashes.

FROM OUTREACH TO OPPORTUNITY: HOW I GOT MY FIRST REAL CLIENT

Two years after I had been let go from Netflix, I was ready to take back my real name and step into the next phase of my business. I wanted to build this with more intention, more ownership, and a clear vision.

I started cold-DMing executives on LinkedIn—leaders at well-known brands and high-end businesses, where every interaction had to feel polished, effortless, and aligned with the image their customers paid a premium for. That was the level that I wanted to operate at and the standard I was determined to build my business around.

After dozens of ignored messages, I finally got a meeting with a former manager from Condé Nast, who had just launched his own marketing firm in Japan.

I took a breath and said something that felt like both a stretch and a vow.

"I have a team. We offer language services that solve real problems for high-end clients. Your clients don't just need accurate translation; they need interpreters who are poised, adaptable, and capable of representing their voices in high-stakes environments."

He leaned in, interested. He told me he had worked with language vendors before. Many were highly skilled but lacked flexibility. They were often too academic or too removed from the realities of fast-paced, client-facing business.

I nodded. "I'm building something different. Service that is elegant, flexible, and professional. Premium communication delivered with humility and meticulous care."

A few weeks later, he hired me to accompany his client to *Adweek* in New York. That one assignment turned into a multi-year translation project for a UK-based trends intelligence firm.

THE CREATION OF GOLD SPEAK, INC.

After the *Adweek* job in 2017, I had proof of concept that my business could work. So, I started my own company, Gold Speak, Inc., as a global communications agency specializing in high-end interpretation and translation.

From there, I continued to introduce myself as an agency owner to more potential clients at meetups, events, and through LinkedIn DMs, which led to more work. This also came with a lot of pressure because, as the lead interpreter and face of the company, the level of my skills had to be proven first, as trust is earned in real-time through live performance, not on paper.

That realization pushed me to grow, but also exposed where I wasn't ready yet.

Around the same time, I tried expanding into the investment and finance sector. I took on a high-level interpreting assignment for a major firm. The room was fast-moving and filled with dense terminology. Midway through, I felt myself falling behind. By the end of the meeting, I was told that parts of my interpretation had missed key components.

The feedback was hard to hear, but it taught me something important. If I wanted to grow this business, it couldn't just be about chasing opportunity. It had to be about alignment between what I was offering and what I was truly equipped to deliver at the highest level.

So I doubled down. I refined my positioning and focused on the industries where I could genuinely thrive. And in the background, I kept learning, quietly building the knowledge and experience I'd need to expand when the time was right.

At the same time, I didn't want to build a big agency. I wanted to build a trusted network. So I called on skilled interpreters who shared the same values I did: grace under pressure, flexible professionalism, and a quiet commitment to client success. I didn't choose them lightly. Every interpreter I work with is someone I trust in the room with my best client, not just for their skill, but for their integrity, presence, and ability to adapt without ego.

We're a small team by design. A tight-knit group of elite professionals who hold ourselves to the highest standard, not because someone demands it, but because we take pride in the craft.

And as the founder, I made a promise from day one: I would treat every interpreter the way I would want to be treated, with respect and appreciation for the art of what we do.

That's how Gold Speak, Inc. took shape. Today, it's a global communications agency serving leaders across high-end retail, creative design, media, architecture, IT, finance, investment (yes, I made it there), and more. A multi-six-figure business that runs lean and profitably, without cold outreach or a traditional sales team.

But the revenue isn't the headline here. The real story is what it took to get here. No viral success. No overnight breakthrough. Not even social media posts or a flashy website. Just the decision to keep showing up—quietly, skillfully, and with the kind of conviction that doesn't need to shout.

That's what it means to be gracefully unbreakable. Not loud, but intentional and steady; always improving, especially when no one's watching.

SERVICE OVER SPOTLIGHT

Building Gold Speak wasn't about becoming a public figure. I wasn't trying to grow a personal brand or become a thought leader. I simply wanted to serve well and to deliver excellence in moments that mattered, even if everything was only behind the scenes. And over time, those quiet moments began to speak louder than any post or headline ever could.

There was a time when I was called last minute to coordinate an interpreter for a high-stakes, cross-border assignment involving a Fortune 500 executive. A global law firm had reached out, urgently needing someone who could handle an exceptionally sensitive task overseas. I couldn't go myself, so I called a trusted interpreter from my small circle. I was grateful that she immediately adjusted her schedule to allow for the assignment. I coordinated her flight, managed communications with the client, handled her layovers and last-minute logistics—including a missing e-ticket that nearly derailed everything.

She arrived just in time. Her interpretation was flawless. The mission was completed. And the client was grateful.

There was no photo, no post, no proof to the outside world. But that was the point. This is what real trust looks like. It's earned in silence, not in spectacle.

SHINAYAKA

There's a word in Japanese that has stayed with me through every chapter of this story: Shinayaka.

Shinayaka means supple, flexible, graceful—yet unbreakable. Like bamboo bending in a storm but never snapping: quietly resilient. Present, but never overpowering.

At first, I didn't realize I was living by this philosophy. I was just doing what I had to do. Adapting, pivoting, and staying grounded while the winds of life pulled at me from all sides.

But now I see it. This has always been my way.

Shinayaka is why I didn't disappear after Netflix.

It's why I could rebuild my business, not from noise or followers, but from presence and trust.

It's why I don't force things. I listen, adjust, and move with intention. It's how I lead, how I cast interpreters for high-stakes meetings, and how I show up for clients who need calm in moments that count.

For most of my life, I thought being "in between" made me weak.

Too Western to be fully accepted in Japanese corporate culture.

Too Eastern to speak up the way my international peers did.

Too quiet to lead. Too soft to succeed.

But Shinayaka taught me something else: being in between isn't a weakness. It's a bridge.

It's the reason clients trust us in rooms where they can't afford to be misunderstood, and maintaining a delicate balance between different cultures is everything that matters.

I'm not less because I don't fit perfectly in one world. I'm more because I've learned to live and lead in both.

And *that* is what it means to be gracefully unbreakable. Not because you push harder, shout louder, or power through. But because you bend, you listen, and you adapt. And still, you don't break.

To my beautiful reader, if you're still reading this and see any part of yourself in these words—if you've ever felt too quiet, too different, or caught between worlds—know this:

Your voice is not too small. Your story is not over.

You don't need to shout to lead or fit perfectly to belong.

You are already skilled in the ways that matter most.

And now it's your turn to rise, to lead, and to build something extraordinary of your own.

Gracefully, on your terms, in your own time.

This is your moment to become unbreakable.

Shinayaka isn't weakness—it's a new kind of strength.

What It Means to Be Shinayaka

Grace Under Fire:
Remaining calm and composed in challenging situations

Adaptability: Being flexible and open to change

Poise + Strength: Combining elegance with resilience

Bicultural Bridge: Connecting Eastern and Western perspectives

Presence Over Noise:
Emphasizing quiet confidence and mindfulness

Emily Kamata is a Japanese–English conference interpreter, agency founder, and quiet leadership advocate who has built a thriving interpretation business by bridging cultures with grace and precision. After an unexpected layoff from a corporate role, she rebuilt her identity, her confidence, and her company from the ground up, founding Gold Speak Inc., a boutique Tokyo-based language service agency trusted by global leaders in luxury, finance, design, technology, and other industries.

Drawing on twenty-five years of experience in high-stakes bilingual communication, Emily now speaks and writes on themes of reinvention, quiet power, and the often-invisible art of building trust across cultures. She is especially passionate about supporting professionals who feel caught between worlds—linguistically, culturally, or emotionally—and helping them discover strength in their quiet.

Her current work includes shaping an intimate global community for women with untold stories and sharing insights that connect deeply across language and identity.

∼

To connect with Emily:

LinkedIn: LinkedIn – Emily Kamata

———

Instagram: Instagram (personal): @emilyspeaksgold

———

Email: emily@gold-speak.com

———

https://www.gold-speak.com/

THE CATALYST: LIFE CHANGING NEWS—FINDING OUT

BY FREIDELEEN (FREDDY) LOU

Knowing that you are at risk for breast cancer is unsettling. Finding out you have it is surreal.

I can remember the moment exactly. As I stood there getting a mammogram, I glanced over to see the scans that were being taken by the radiology tech. The image was irrefutable. The brightness of the mass that was causing me so much pain was definitely... something. Dare I say it? Silent and concerned, I mentally prepared myself for the words that I feared would come next.

The appointment was in two parts; the next was the ultrasound. As the tech ran the wand over my breasts, I could see dark masses, which confirmed that there was some type of growth. The tech gets ready to make a call but says, "This is standard procedure that we do for everyone. I always call the doctor in the middle of taking the ultrasound just to make sure I got pictures and measurements of everything they wanted." As I tried half-heartedly to believe her, the radiologist came in to discuss the results.

Then came those very words I knew would come. "You have cancer."

There was nothing to do but silently accept it and let the tears fall. The words sunk in, hitting me like a ton of bricks. Then so many emotions coursed through my veins—fear, despair, anger, sadness, worry. After a minute or two, I mustered the strength and said, "So what happens now?"

The radiologist explained that two biopsies would be done: one for the breast and a second for the abnormal lymph node found. So I was seated outside, waiting to be taken for the biopsies. Silently crying, I texted my husband, Marc, that the appointment was not great. Due to the spotty service in the basement, I wasn't sure if it even went through before the oncologist arrived.

The oncologist was empathetic and asked if I had been shown the scans yet. I said, "No," and he brought me in to see the scans more clearly. As he explained the findings in detail, answered my questions, and explained the next step, a biopsy. He put me at ease a bit.

Resigned, we went up to do the biopsies. After a couple of pricks, the samples were gathered. The oncologist walked me back and addressed additional questions, again putting me somewhat at ease.

As I left my appointment with this diagnosis, knowing that this was my new reality, all I could think of was, *How is this going to impact the family?*

THE DRIVE HOME AND TELLING THE FAMILY

As I walked sullenly to the car, red-eyed, my mind continuously racing about what just happened... the impact on my family... my young kids, ages 4 and 3 years old. *Why me? What did I do? What didn't I do right?*

After taking some time, I drove home, tears constantly falling, knowing that when I got home, I could not/should not show them. I had to be the rock for my family, the kids. Would it be enough? Could I handle it?

As I entered the door, I put on the bravest face I could as my kids ran up to me. My heart was bursting with so much love for my kids, and my mind started to race again about all of the what-ifs. I quietly told myself to stop and enjoy the moment. I held my boys tightly, so full of love.

Then I saw my husband, Marc, in the living room. There were no words to explain the apprehension that I saw in his eyes. As we ushered the kids to their play area, we went to have a heart-to-heart. As I said those words again—"I have cancer"—the tears started to fall. Marc was silent. He immediately said, "You're going to be okay." At that very moment, I knew that he would be my rock no matter what.

As I broke the news to my immediate family, the spoken words were consistently positive. They reiterated how strong I was and how I could overcome anything. The positivity was extremely overwhelming as I was just processing... or trying to. Honestly, I just didn't want to hear it. My mindset was not in the right space. They weren't doing anything wrong; it was just that, on so many levels, they didn't understand what I was going through. Despite it all, I continued to put on a brave face in public, knowing that emotionally I was a huge broken mess.

With all the thoughts going through my mind, I kept coming back to what was first and foremost: my family.

As a wife and mother to two young boys, you wonder what life will be like and how you will do anything and everything to make sure that you are there with them.

The results indicated that we caught it early, which was great. The bad news was that my type usually has recurrence within five years due to several factors. The size of the mass was large, so a mastectomy was definitely necessary. Since it was hormone receptor positive, medication would be necessary to keep it under control. Chemotherapy and radiation treatments were yet to be determined.

So after getting all this information, all I thought of was:

- *What is the likelihood that this will come back?*
- *How can I mitigate risk?*
- *What is the recovery time?*
- *How will it impact how active I am with kids?*
- *Who is going to watch the kids as I recover?*
- and so much more...

Crazy how life changes in an instant. But we find our strength with those we love. I decided to stay positive despite sporadic tears!

WHAT NO ONE TELLS YOU ABOUT CANCER

The truth is, even if you have an inkling that you may have cancer, it impacts you. But as soon as you hear those six letters, C-A-N-C-E-R, your life is forever changed. There is no going back because the emotional weight of those words creates such a void in your heart and your person in your body.

The thing is, everyone means well and wants to be positive on your behalf. But in truth, it was very exhausting. It was exhausting having to be positive to show them that you had it all together... to constantly put on a brave face and not be allowed to be vulnerable... to process the real emotions that were raging inside. So I found an outlet.

A site called CaringBridge was my outlet. It gave me a space to journal and write what was really going on, if I chose to show it and express it. Because when it came down to it, despite the immense support that I had from my family, friends, and community, I felt so alone. The emotions that I was feeling were so immense, and not being able to express them to truly let it out only made things worse. I needed to be able to process it; instead, I was keeping it at bay in front of people. All I could do was keep moving forward.

Cancer is definitely no laughing matter. But to my surprise, there was one moment when it was. Can you imagine going into an appointment with your general surgeon and oncologist, knowing that you will be talking about your treatment plan because of cancer, and laughing? Well, it was truly surprising to me, too.

Who wouldn't be apprehensive about going to this type of appointment? I'll admit that I was. I had two pages of questions ready to be asked and answered. I'm a planner (read: worrier), so I needed to know before, during, and after what to expect, possible surprises, recurrence rate, pre-op treatment, post-op treatment, and much more. Of course, not all answers are as clear-cut as I would've liked, but you take what you can get to make the best-informed decision.

So why the laughing? Well, I'm blessed to have a smart-ass husband who knows how to lighten the mood. Without going into too much detail, we were talking about breast augmentation/reconstruction. He's definitely my perfect match, as he balances out my seriousness.

On a serious note: Every person has a right to make choices for what is best in their lives. But what if certain choices were taken away from you?

When I was dealt the cancer card, I didn't realize the impact that it would have when it came down to family planning. How would you feel if you were told that you couldn't have any more children? Or that you would have to delay it for five to ten years?

That's the situation that I found myself in. Being no spring chicken and having kids late, I pretended to accept the news for what it was when I was in the doctor's office. But the real deal is... I'm *not* okay with it.

Am I selfish?

Am I stupid?

Am I ungrateful?

As I expressed these concerns to my support group, I found that I wasn't alone. To answer the three questions above, we are none of that. But we find ourselves in a situation where we feel like it.

As women, we are already robbed of something that makes us feminine: our breasts. And yes, reconstruction is an option, but it's not the same because we literally had (or will have) a piece or pieces cut from our bodies. We truly lose a part of ourselves.

So I struggled with the reality that having a third child may not be an option, and I counted my blessings that I have two handsome boys.

Having this choice taken away due to the future treatment, I wasn't okay with it. I'd never be okay with it. But who knows, a little blessing may arrive despite all odds.

BREAKING THE SILENCE: DECEMBER 2018

It had been months since my diagnosis when I finally felt the nudge to speak publicly. Up until then, I had gone quiet on social media—not out of shame, but because I needed space to process everything. My world had shifted, and I wasn't ready to put that into words. But in December 2018, something changed. I felt a pull to share, to explain why I had disappeared, and maybe—just maybe—help someone else feel less alone.

During that time, I had started journaling. It wasn't a perfect fix, but it gave me a small sense of control—something to hold onto when the chaos in my life felt overwhelming. Putting my thoughts on paper helped me release some of the weight I was carrying. It didn't make the pain disappear, but it helped me move forward, even if just one page at a time.

Eventually, I took what I had written and turned it into something I could speak. I hit "Go Live" on Facebook, heart racing, hoping I wouldn't fall apart.

I thought I was brave. I thought I could power through my message without breaking down. But as soon as I started talking, the weight of it all came flooding out. I cried... I managed to make it through, albeit teary-eyed. The emotions had been building for so long, and speaking my truth aloud made them impossible to contain. Cancer wasn't just something happening to my body—it had woven itself into my identity. Saying the words out loud made it real.

But what happened next was something I never expected.

Messages began pouring in—friends, acquaintances, even distant connections. Many had walked a similar road but had never said a word. They, too, had gone silent. Some shared heartbreaking stories of being abandoned by partners or unsupported by family. Others said they stayed quiet because they didn't think anyone would understand.

That day, my Facebook Live did more than update people—it opened a door. A door to healing, to connection, and to community. And that was the moment I realized that my voice mattered. My story had a purpose.

And if speaking up helped even one person feel less alone, then I would never stay silent again.

THE INSURANCE GAP

Have you ever heard of the *what-ifs* of life? Well, my situation is definitely one of them. Two months before my diagnosis, my husband and I were more focused on future financial family planning and looking into life insurance. After meeting with several different agents, we found that the options being provided were all very standard, kind of like our parents' life insurance: It made it seem like you just pay to die. So we continued our search, and then the inevitable happened... I was diagnosed. Who knew it would take that long to find a policy that we would like, only for it to be too late for me to get it? Once diagnosed, you fall into the *what-ifs*... the *coulda/shoulda/woulda* situation. And in the world of life insurance, you fall into a waiting period where you become UNINSURABLE. It really highlighted the unpredictability of life because *what-if* moments stem from hindsight. I realized that an earlier choice could have changed things drastically. If I had secured life insurance before the diagnosis, things could have been financially different. The thought was unsettling.

What made it even more frustrating is that we were so close to a different outcome. We were already looking into it. We didn't know what was coming, and we hesitated on making a decision. Then, of course, life threw us a curveball. We didn't make the wrong choice, but the fact that we didn't make it at the right time was painfully ironic.

So the conundrum is that an insurance gap exists when it comes to timing and eligibility. Because life insurance policies require applicants to disclose their medical history, once a serious diagnosis like cancer enters the picture, securing coverage becomes more difficult, more expensive, or even impossible.

Because we hadn't locked in a policy yet, the moment my diagnosis happened led insurers to reassess risk, resulting in exclusions or outright denial. It's definitely a frustrating situation where proactive steps could have made a difference, but you just never know until it happens. No one ever expects bad news until it's too late.

DISCOVERING LIVING BENEFITS

After my surgery, I was recovering from a double mastectomy. Doctors indicated that this was a very aggressive approach to handle stage 0 DCIS, but I had my reasons. As a wife and mother to two young boys, ages 4 and 3, I needed to be aggressive for them. I needed to ensure that I was mitigating any possible future risk of recurrence.

Despite being in recovery, my search for life insurance still continued. It was at this point in time that my sister introduced me to **Indexed Universal Life (IUL) insurance with Living Benefits**. She wasn't well-versed, so she introduced me to someone who could explain it to me. Let's just say my mind was blown; it shifted everything that I thought I knew. It was the product that I didn't know I was searching for when we were initially looking for life insurance.

So, what is **Indexed Universal Life (IUL) and Living Benefits?**

It is a powerful combination that offers flexibility, wealth-building potential, and lifelong protection. It is an amazing option for those looking to secure their financial future while gaining access to living benefits to protect their families and live life.

IUL is a permanent life insurance policy that not only provides a death benefit but also includes a cash value component that grows over time. This allows policyholders to potentially earn higher returns compared to traditional whole life insurance without being directly exposed to market losses.

PAIRING IUL WITH LIVING BENEFITS

Living Benefits within IUL policies take life insurance beyond just protection—they provide **financial support while you're still alive**, offering coverage for:

- **Critical Illness:** Helps cover medical expenses and lost income during events like heart attacks, strokes, or cancer treatment. A sudden health crisis can bring overwhelming medical bills and lost income. Living Benefits help ease that burden.
- **Chronic Illness:** Provides funds for long-term care services when daily activities become challenging. Long-term care can be incredibly expensive, whether it's home health services or assisted living. These benefits can provide support when daily tasks become difficult.
- **Terminal Illness:** Allows policyholders to access **tax-free funds** to ease financial stress and focus on meaningful experiences in their final months. When a doctor estimates less than 12–24 months of life expectancy, access to funds allows policyholders to focus on what matters: spending quality time with loved ones, arranging affairs, or even fulfilling final wishes.

FREEDOM IN HOW YOU USE THE BENEFITS

Once a claim is exercised, funds can be used however you need:

- **Covering medical expenses** beyond traditional health insurance.
- **Supporting your family** with childcare, home expenses, or tuition.
- **Enjoying meaningful experiences** by taking a trip with loved ones.

IUL with living benefits is a smarter approach to life insurance

Unlike traditional policies that only pay out upon death, Indexed Universal Life combines long-term financial security with Living Benefits, ensuring policyholders can protect their families while maintaining financial independence.

After having my mind completely blown about this amazing product, I came to learn a couple of things:

1. It is not a new product; it has been around for decades.
2. Not a lot of people know about this product.
3. A lot of people think that the only life insurance option is to pay to die, not to live.

When I asked my fellow peers in a similar stage of life with young families, I came to realize that we did not know as much as we thought we did. The old way of saving is not the way to go. There are newer, better methods to maximize or create generational wealth, to protect your family, and to mitigate the *what-ifs..*

WHAT LIVING BENEFITS ACTUALLY COVER

The old way of insurance—the traditional way—is that your beneficiary gets paid when you die. The benefit of the policy lies with your beneficiary, serving you no purpose while you're still alive. Traditional life insurance serves as a financial safety net for loved ones after you're gone—but what if your needs arise while you're still here, navigating life's toughest seasons?

The new way of insurance includes Living Benefits which allow you, as the owner and policyholder, to be alive to reap some of those benefits. **Living Benefits shift the focus from merely providing for others after death to ensuring you have financial security when life takes unexpected turns.**

Living Benefits redefine the purpose of life insurance, shifting the focus from what happens after death to how it can provide security and support while you're still here. These benefits ensure that policyholders have financial resources available when facing some of life's most challenging moments.

A Lifeline When Life Gets Hard. We all need them, and like most, we don't want to go to others for help. Living Benefits don't just help you recover after hardship—they provide resources during it. Whether you're facing a serious illness, struggling with long-term care costs, or preparing for retirement, these benefits offer flexibility, protection, and peace of mind when you need them most. Think of it like a personal GoFundMe.

Beyond a Policy—Building a Plan for Life. Living Benefits isn't just about insurance; it's a strategic financial tool. It can be more than protection—it can become your legacy.

With Living Benefits, your policy can function as:

- **A College Fund:** Setting aside resources for your children's education.
- **A Wedding Fund:** Supporting milestones for the next generation.
- **A Business Fund:** Investing in opportunities, entrepreneurship, and financial independence.
- **A Car Fund:** Making major purchases more manageable.
- **A Retirement Plan / Self-Funded Pension:** Supplementing future income without relying solely on traditional retirement accounts.
- **An Emergency Fund:** Ensuring financial stability when life throws unexpected challenges your way.
- **And More...**

Why Living Benefits Matter: While traditional insurance is about paying to die, Living Benefits ensure you're financially empowered to live. You deserve the ability to navigate life's uncertainties with confidence, protect your loved ones, and create a meaningful financial foundation—both for yourself and those who come after you.

The bonus is that it is a **Financial Safety Net Without Restrictions.** The funds received through Living Benefits are tax-free, and there are no limitations on how the money is used, whether you need it for:

- **Childcare:** Ensuring stability for your family during challenging times.
- **Out-of-network medical treatment:** Accessing specialists or treatments beyond standard insurance coverage.
- **A once-in-a-lifetime experience:** Making meaningful memories with loved ones instead of being financially constrained.

Unlike traditional life insurance, these benefits offer flexibility and empower policyholders to make decisions that prioritize their well-being today, not just after they're gone.

"Once a claim is exercised, it's yours to use without limits." This guarantee ensures that your benefits truly work for you when you need them most.

LICENSED + ON A MISSION (MAY 2019)

From Recovery to Purpose—How Urgency Led to a Mission: Even while still recovering from surgery, I couldn't ignore the urgency I felt. It wasn't just about my own situation anymore—it was about the countless families who, just like mine, were unknowingly vulnerable. The more I thought about it, the more it nagged at me.

I started asking friends and family about their awareness of **Living Benefits**, and the answers shocked me to my core. **95–98 percent of them had no idea such protections existed.** The few who did—only about 2–5 percent—were life insurance agents, agency owners, or financial advisors. But their responses frustrated me even more: They knew, yet they never talked about it simply because they didn't sell those policies. How infuriating this was to learn!

One agency owner even dismissed **Indexed Universal Life (IUL) with Living Benefits** altogether, calling it "a rip-off." That's when I learned about captive agents—those who could only sell what their company allowed them to. But even if they couldn't sell certain products, they could have educated people about them. Yet they didn't. That realization hit hard —it showed me just how deep the gap was in the insurance industry, and how families were unknowingly suffering for it.

Turning Idleness into Action. I've never been one to sit still, even in recovery. I knew I needed to take care of myself, but at the same time, I felt **an undeniable urgency** to protect my family and share what I had learned with others. Instead of sitting idle, I put that time to work—I **studied, got licensed, and turned my fear into purpose.**

By **May 2019**, I became **licensed and ready**—not just to sell insurance, but to **educate and guide families** through proper financial planning. This wasn't just about selling policies; it was about **empowering people** with knowledge and financial literacy they had never been given before.

Educating Communities—One Conversation at a Time. Along with my team, I started hosting home meetings and small group presentations, bringing together families to teach them how to protect themselves. We partnered with small business owners, showing them how to secure their livelihoods in case the inevitable happened. Individuals, families, and businesses—all of them needed access to these *highly unused benefits* that could change their financial futures.

This was more than just transactions. **We weren't just selling insurance. We were planting seeds.**

A Legacy of Knowledge. We understood that knowledge is power, and that's what we were sharing. It wasn't about making a sale—it was about providing education, resources, and real solutions that would allow families to do what was best for them with proper planning.

Through financial literacy, we were shifting mindsets, challenging outdated industry norms, and planting the seeds for families to grow into financial security, independence, and generational wealth.

And that mission? It's still growing today.

LIMITLESS IMPACT

SECOND DIAGNOSIS: ROUND TWO (JULY 2022)

In January 2021, our hearts were filled with overwhelming joy as we welcomed our first and only baby girl into the world—a blessing we never thought possible. Doctors said that with my age, diagnosis, and the need for long-term hormone therapy—anywhere from five to ten years—getting pregnant again might not happen. But faith, hope, and love had other plans, and we welcomed our little miracle.

We were basking in the sweetness of family life: raising three kids, including our beautiful daughter. Life finally felt light again... until it didn't.

It was July 2022. After celebrating a fun-filled Fourth of July with the family, I bent down to buckle my then 18-month-old into her car seat, and a sharp, searing pain struck my chest. It stopped me in my tracks. I instantly knew something was wrong. It was that same unmistakable pain that haunted me during my first battle with cancer.

I went straight to the doctor. The tests followed. And then the words that shook my soul all over again: "You have cancer."

This time, it was **Stage 2**.

The news shattered me.

Why me?

Why again?

Hadn't I been through enough?

A year-plus of treatment began, putting my body through the ringer. My plan included a lumpectomy, followed by chemotherapy, radiation, and ongoing hormone therapy. Each phase chipped away at me physically and emotionally. I experienced excruciating back pain, dry mouth, migraines, extreme fatigue, weight changes, loss of appetite, hair loss, and more. Every part of me ached—some days in ways I couldn't even describe.

One of the hardest parts? The mom guilt. The fatigue meant I often couldn't play with my kids. I'd hear them giggling from the other room, and all I could do was lie there, exhausted, broken, guilty. The emotional rollercoaster of treatment caused unpredictable mood swings. Despite knowing they were side effects, nothing prepared me for the heartbreak of snapping at my children or yelling when I didn't mean to. In those moments, I felt like I was failing them, and it crushed me.

THE CATALYST: LIFE CHANGING NEWS—FINDING OUT

I tried to hide the worst parts from them. I still showed up when I could, even if just to read a story from the couch. But those scary mom moments weighed heavily on me.

On **April 15, 2025**, I officially entered **Survivorship**. While I still undergo regular check-ins and hormone therapy, I am no longer in active treatment. It's a strange place—grateful and relieved, but still carrying fear tucked into quiet corners of my heart.

Still, this chapter reminds me: I've done this before. I hope that I don't have to go through this again, but if I have to, I will.

Because now I know: *I am stronger than I ever imagined.*

THIS TIME WAS DIFFERENT—YOU WERE COVERED

They say blessings come in many forms. For me, during one of the most terrifying moments of my life, that blessing came not only through the love and support of my family, friends, and community, but through the power of being *prepared*.

This time, we were covered.

I had two life insurance policies in place, each with a $250,000 death benefit and critical illness protection. We weren't expecting to need them so soon, but when I was diagnosed, we knew it was time to file a **Living Benefits** claim.

To our relief, one of the policies was active and eligible. The other, unfortunately, had lapsed. I had originally held over $1 million in coverage split between a term life policy and an indexed universal life (IUL) policy. But like many families, we underestimated the *"what-ifs"* and let a major portion of that protection go. That was a hard lesson, but one I share today so others don't make the same mistake: **Always overprotect. You never know when you'll need it.**

Thankfully, our active IUL policy provided what we needed most in that moment: *relief*.

We were approved for a **Living Benefits payout of over $120,000—tax-free**. That allowed me to step away from work, focus entirely on healing, and still keep our household afloat.

What many people don't realize is how devastating the financial burden of a critical illness can be. It's not just the cost of treatment—it's the impact on your entire family. The stress of mounting bills, missed work, and decisions made out of desperation can delay healing or even prevent someone from seeking treatment at all.

I was reminded of this harsh truth when I learned about a friend's sister. She hid a recurrence of cancer from her loved ones because she didn't want to put her family through the financial strain again. The weight of *money* kept her from asking for help. No one should ever have to choose between *healing* and *hardship*.

But Living Benefits can change that. Whether it's using the funds to pursue experimental treatment, cover out-of-network care, or simply spend precious time with loved ones, this benefit creates space to *live*.

When my family received that payout, I realized something profound: *I had become the product of the product.* And with that realization came a responsibility—to share what I knew. So when I had the strength, even during treatment, I began creating educational resources for my community. I knew others needed to hear this.

Because no one should have to choose between their *life* and their *livelihood*, this peace of mind—this freedom—is beyond measure.

"It gave me serenity in the storm."

GIVE THEM SOMETHING TO WALK AWAY WITH: THE FAMILY FUTURE FRAMEWORK

Your 5-Step Path from Clarity to Legacy

Every journey starts with a single decision. For me, it began with a diagnosis that shattered everything familiar. Twice. Cancer didn't just test my body—it tested my spirit, my motherhood, my faith, and my purpose. In that fire, I found clarity: I was meant to rise, not just for myself, but for others who feel lost, overwhelmed, or stuck in fear. That's how *Fear to Purpose* was born. That's why *Family Future Legacy Insurance* and *Family Future Legacy* exist today—not just as services, but as movements.

I know how it feels to sit at the kitchen table, heart racing, wondering if you've done enough to protect your family if the unthinkable happens. I've sat in that chair, both as the patient and the provider. That's why I created *The Family Future Framework* —a simple, five-step path to help you move from confusion to clarity and from fear to legacy.

THE CATALYST: LIFE CHANGING NEWS—FINDING OUT

Step 1: Check Your Readiness

Take a moment to reflect. What do you have in place right now to protect your family financially? Do you know what would happen if illness, loss, or hardship showed up unexpectedly? Ignoring it won't make it go away, but checking your readiness *will* give you power.

- **Download** the "Fear To Purpose | Client Journey & Readiness Checklist"
- **Download** the "Fear To Purpose | Client Readiness Checklist"

Step 2: Talk With Your Loved Ones

Have the uncomfortable conversations. Talk about your dreams, your fears, and your responsibilities. Avoiding the topic of life insurance, critical illness coverage, or legacy planning doesn't protect anyone—it just delays peace of mind. Let love guide the conversation.

- It's Never Easy to Talk About the Future
- Life Insurance Can Be Life-Changing

Step 3: Watch the Info Video

These quick videos break things down without the jargon or pressure. They are designed for real people, real families, real situations—because that's who I serve.

- Insuring a Long Life is More Than A Policy
- Changing the Life of People With Diabetes

Step 4: Complete Your Financial Fitness Check-Up

It's not about being perfect—it's about knowing where you stand. Our free tool gives you a snapshot of your financial protection, no strings attached. It's like a checkup for your legacy, helping you plan with confidence and clarity.

- **Complete** the Financial Fitness Check-Up

Step 5: Take Action & Join the Movement

The time is now. Book a consultation. Share the video. Start the conversation. Join a community of everyday people choosing to protect what matters most. This isn't just about policies—it's about purpose, peace of mind, and people who care.

You've read my story. Now it's time to write your next chapter. Let this be the moment where you choose legacy over fear. You don't have to walk this journey alone—we're here, and we're ready when you are.

- **Book your meeting** today to get started (Calendly Link: https://bit.ly/FFLClientConsultation)
- **Join our Group:**
- **Fear To Purpose**
- **Family Future Legacy Group**

Because the truth is simple:
Hope is a decision. Protection is a plan. Legacy is a choice.

Your Mission Statement:

"Turning pain into purpose by inspiring lives, empowering communities, and protecting futures—one story, one family, one legacy at a time."

Your Brand Structure:

- **@FearToPurpose** – For women rising from grief, illness, or hardship
- **@FamilyFutureLegacy (Nonprofit)** – Community events, workshops, school partnerships (#FFLcares)
- **@FamilyFutureLegacyInsurance** – Financial literacy, policy review, family financial planning, protection products, income opportunities for families & businesses

Call to Action:

Your journey doesn't end with survival — it begins with purpose. Whether you're looking to protect your family, earn income with impact, or gain financial clarity—you are not alone.

Take your next step toward purpose:

- **Download** the "Fear To Purpose | Client Journey & Readiness Checklist"
- **Download** the "Fear To Purpose | Client Readiness Checklist"
- **Complete** the Financial Fitness Check-Up
- **Book your meeting** today to get started (Calendly Link: https://bit.ly/FFLClientConsultation)

Your future is worth it. Your purpose is calling. Let's build your legacy—together.

I didn't choose cancer. I didn't choose the fear, the pain, the uncertainty, or the nights I spent wondering if I'd be there to raise my children or if I would overcome this health challenge. But I *did* choose what to do with it. I chose to turn my pain into purpose. That choice has led me here—to you.

"Turning pain into purpose by inspiring lives, empowering communities, and protecting futures—one story, one family, one legacy at a time."

This isn't just a mission statement—it's the reason I wake up every day. From my personal battle with cancer to the financial stress that threatened to steal our peace, I know what it means to fight for more than just survival. And I know what it takes to rise.

That's why I created three purpose-driven platforms, all anchored in one mission—to help families and individuals rise with clarity, strength, and legacy.

The Family Future Brand Structure

- **@FearToPurpose** is for those who've been through the fire—grief, illness, loss, or any hardship that left them feeling broken. This space is your reminder: you are not broken; you are *becoming*.

- **@FamilyFutureLegacy** is our nonprofit arm, where we show up for families through school partnerships, community outreach, and seasonal drives. Whether it's food, resources, or hope—we deliver what's needed. **#FFLcares**

- **@FamilyFutureLegacyInsurance** equips families with the tools to protect what matters most—through policy education, legacy planning, and income opportunities for those ready to serve with heart.

Each platform is connected by purpose and built with you in mind.

YOUR NEXT STEP TOWARD PURPOSE

You've read the story. Maybe parts of it felt familiar. Now it's time to move from inspiration to action. Because your journey doesn't end with surviving—it *starts* when you choose to build with purpose.

Here's how to get started:

- **Download** the "Fear To Purpose | Client Journey & Readiness Checklist"
- **Download** the "Fear To Purpose | Client Readiness Checklist"

- **Complete** your Financial Fitness Check-Up—a free, no-pressure way to see where you stand

- **Book your meeting** today to get started (Calendly Link: https://bit.ly/FFLClientConsultation)

THE CATALYST: LIFE CHANGING NEWS—FINDING OUT

You don't have to have it all figured out. You just have to take the next step.

Your future is worth it. Your purpose is calling.
Let's build your legacy—together.

〜

Freideleen Lou founded Family Future Legacy Insurance Agency and the nonprofit Family Future Legacy, leveraging her personal experience as a breast cancer survivor (October 2018, July 2022) and executive leadership to educate families on financial resilience and legacy building. Before founding her agency in 2019, she built a diverse career across banking, finance, commercial real estate, startups, and franchising—scaling a beverage brand from 5 to 50 locations in one year. Her approach is grounded in empathy, hard-earned experience, and a clear mission: helping others navigate unexpected challenges with strategy, security, and purpose.

〜

To watch Freideleen's Facebook Live:

https://www.facebook.com/reel/673655798466833

SHE ROSE ANYWAY
BY KELLEY WEINZETL

Hello, my name is Kelley Weinzetl; I am a married mama of two, a daughter of God, an entrepreneur, and a dreamer chasing down her dreams. I was born in Southern California and raised in a small town called Cowiche, Washington. After high school, I attended Yakima Community College to play basketball and soccer. As a college athlete, I led a wild life. I was not making good choices and was barely scraping by with my grades. The choices I made ended with me becoming a pregnant teenager. I was 19 years old, and after recognizing some odd symptoms, I decided to take a pregnancy test; lo and behold, I was pregnant. I seriously thought my life was over!

I can remember that day as if it happened yesterday. I had purchased a pregnancy test from the store and, for some reason, ended up taking it in a Starbucks bathroom. I bawled my eyes out all the way home, thinking my life was over. All I could see for myself was a life of poverty, and all of my dreams and aspirations were now flushed down the toilet.

I have always been pro-life, but now that I was confronted with pregnancy at a young age and clearly not prepared for the consequences of my decisions, I found myself contemplating my position. To make a long story short, I decided not only to have my baby but also to rise up and be the mom she deserved. It was not her fault that I was irresponsible, and I didn't trust anyone to know how to raise my daughter right, except me. I remember the shame I felt when I finally told my family I was pregnant. It was as if the veil that was hiding all of my promiscuous choices was lifted, and I was left naked in front of them. After a few weeks of struggling with this, it finally hit me that I don't know when I will be pregnant again or if I will ever have another child, so I'd better enjoy this time to the fullest. That mindset shift allowed me to enjoy every second of my pregnancy.

Thankfully, I had an easy pregnancy, and my daughter was born healthy.

My daughter's father and I were together for about four years. I expected to spend the rest of my life with him; we had discussed marriage and all the things that lay ahead. Unfortunately, he decided he no longer wanted our relationship, and on December 18th, 2010, I became a single mother. I was in pure shock, and it was the rock-bottom moment of my life. I am pretty sure I had a panic attack—it was an out-of-body experience, like I was watching myself go through this painful moment. This night was ranked as the worst night of my life, but now that I am on the other side, I can say for certain that my worst night has become my best night.

Once the dust settled, I realized I had some very important choices to make, and I was presented with some pretty embarrassing realities. How was I going to provide a life for my daughter? Would I take him to court? Would I fight for child support? What would visitation look like? I had no idea who I was outside of the relationship. I didn't know what I liked to wear, what my favorite color was, or who I wanted to be. I felt disgusted with myself. Thankfully, right before all of this happened, I had given my life to Jesus! The night my life imploded, I ran, crying my eyes out, to the feet of Jesus, and I stayed there crying for about six months.

Looking back now, those days I spent at the feet of Jesus not only created the foundation of my relationship with Him but also exercised and honed my gift of prayer. As I found myself in prayer, I told God I didn't want to stay in the pain of this moment for the rest of my life. I have seen so many other women who had a child outside of marriage; the relationship didn't work out, and then they lived out of the bitterness of that moment for the rest of their lives. I did not want that to be me!

I told the Lord I wanted Him to heal me from the inside out, to tear apart my wounds and heal me so I would be whole and become the woman I was meant to be in Him. I wanted to heal and move on with life. I decided I would remain single for at least two years to focus on being the mom my daughter deserved, healing, and finishing my schooling. Too many people become single parents, hopping from relationship to relationship, dragging their child or children along with them, and I did not want that for my daughter.

As my journey started, I was tested right away. Two men with whom I had an obvious mutual attraction asked me to come play basketball with them on separate occasions. Even though I wanted to go so badly, I did not, because *I knew that I knew that I knew* how that story would end. I could hear the Holy Spirit telling me not to go. I felt like He was saying if I went, I would end up in the toxic cycle I was fighting to stay out of. Today, I am so thankful I made the choice to stay home. I do not think I would be where I am and who I am if I had chosen to meet up with either of them.

A few months after I became a single mom, I finished my schooling in Yakima and was accepted into the MRI program at BSU. So we made the move to Boise, Idaho, giving us a fresh start. I was no longer on government assistance programs, and I was able to navigate the challenge of custody and financial support outside of court by the grace of God. People would ask me why I didn't collect child support, and I would just respond that God is my provider, not my daughter's father. (Everyone has their own opinion and situation; this was just my own conviction.)

My daughter is now 18 years old; it has been a wild ride, but we have made it! As a young single mom, we grew up together. We made it through some difficult times, but I never gave up; I always kept fighting for tomorrow and for my dreams to come true. I realized early on, when I decided to be single for two years, that I needed to figure out who I wanted to become. In my next relationship, I didn't want to be the same chameleon, changing myself to match who that man wanted me to be. I was designed and destined to be a leading woman, and I could not take the chance of being trapped in another relationship with a man who didn't match who I was and who I would become. I decided to stop waiting for my husband to come along and save us from the circumstances in life. I chose to rise up and be the hero in my own story. The only man I needed in life was Jesus, and I would wait for my husband until the timing was right.

To fast forward to the end, I was single for ten years and nine months. Before I met my now husband, I accomplished every big goal I had prayed about: I was the first in my family to graduate with my bachelor's degree, I paid off $25k and became debt-free, I rose from an entry-level worker to the Chief Operating Officer (which more than doubled my income), I lost 40 lbs—and have kept the weight off! I was not waiting to live my life; I was living my life on my own terms right then and there. After I had accomplished all of these things, I finally met my husband! God has redeemed my family, and we are living our happily ever after.

The reason I am sharing my story is to help women out there who feel like they have made wrong choices and are stuck in life, moms who have had to put their dreams on hold until their children are grown, women that are barely surviving, unsure of how they will even feed their family—I want them to have hope that a thriving life is waiting for them. They just have to choose it and go after it. I want my story to be a beacon of hope to my sisters out there who burn for more but have no idea how it can possibly happen. I want you to see that if I can overcome and be where I am today, anyone can! I am here to cheer you on and lead the way!

I've walked through the fire, overcome every obstacle, and now I'm living the life I once only dreamed of. I want this for all of you! In this chapter, you will learn how I rose up to be the hero of my own story, and that it is never too late to start your comeback story. Jesus is the secret sauce! You'll learn how to make every goal the stepping stone to the next and how to use your words to rewrite your story into the empowering destiny you dream of.

After you read this chapter, I hope you are on fire for the life you have burning in your heart, and you are filled with hope and encouragement that if I can do it, then so can you! I hope that you finally draw the line in the sand and decide, *I choose the life of my dreams, and it starts here and now!* Yes, every choice has to be backed up by action, but it is heartbreaking how many people choose to never choose themselves. Let's change that! It is time to choose the life of your dreams! Don't wait another year, month, week, or day—let's start now! Come on this journey with me and hold on tight!

After I had graduated from BSU and I was in my first condo with my daughter, I remember feeling fearful that I may not be able to pay the bills,

I may not be able to pay rent, and I may not be able to pay for groceries. I was excited for us to be out on our own, and I did trust God to help provide, but I was immature in my faith, and my faith was weak. I felt vulnerable. I had doubts and limiting beliefs that I had not uncovered yet. I remember going on vacation and seeing families that were "whole," making happy memories, taking fun pictures, and seemingly living their best lives. This would make me feel like I needed to wait for us to be a "whole" family before we could do the "big things," or that we were missing out on making memories with the man who was supposed to come into our lives.

After a bit of time passed, I had this very real realization that I had no idea when my husband was coming into my life, so if I continued to wait, life would pass us by, and instead of making memories, we would still just be waiting. It occurred to me that this was unfair to my daughter and me; rather than wasting time waiting, I could be building the life I want to live. I had this misaligned thought process that I needed my husband to show up first, and then we could live the life of our dreams. I thought that to really flourish and thrive, I needed my husband in my life to be the hero that saves us from living paycheck to paycheck, on a very strict budget, and not having extra. Thankfully, Jesus came in and shook those thoughts right out of my head!

I can't remember exactly when it happened, but there was a shift in my life when the reality that I didn't know when my husband was coming into my life met the truth of who I am in Jesus. It changed my life forever. My perspective all of a sudden shifted to understand that actually my family was already whole because Jesus is in my life. He is my husband before my physical husband arrives. He is my Savior who sweeps me off my feet and makes everything right. I didn't have to wait; the man I was waiting for was already in my life, and because of Him, I was already equipped to live the life I dreamed of. I was designed to be the hero of my own story because of my identity in Christ.

When this shift happened, there was no more holding off living my best life; there was no more waiting to make "life plans" for when that other person entered my life. If I were going to get married one day, God would just make him fit into the life I was creating. I wanted to create the life of my dreams, and I didn't want to hold anything back, so I got busy! I am a "go big or go home" type of girl, so once I had the mindset shift, this wasn't very hard. I didn't want to be living a life that I needed to be saved from. I wanted to be in a position where my husband could come in and complement my life.

Now that I am on the other side of this, I can say that because I chose to go after the life of my dreams, took charge to create the life I wanted so badly, the journey of this pursuit turned me into the woman my husband needed me to be when we finally met. If I had sat on my hands and simply waited, I don't think I would have been ready for him, nor do I think he would have been attracted to that woman. I became a confident, dominant, and independent woman—all things that my husband loves about me (most of the time!)

If you find yourself today in the midst of a season of being single, I am talking directly to you. Do not allow yourself to play the damsel in distress, and do not allow yourself to believe you need to have a man in your life to be successful or live the life that fulfills you. God has gifted His daughters with all of the tools they need to create the lives they dream of while they wait for their husbands to finally show up! I want to encourage each and every one of you to rise up and be the hero in your own story, saddle up that horse, and ride in as the white knight we have all been taught is coming to save us. You are the white knight; you are the hero in the story! Your husband is not coming to save you; the only one who gets that pressure is Jesus, and the great thing is, He already did it! You just have to pick yourself up and get on the saddle; Jesus has already made the way for you. The woman you are designed and destined to become will thank you, and so will the rest of the world. We need each other to live true to who we are designed to be. You never know whose story will be altered by your testimony and by the gifts you have to share. Take your story into your own hands, and with God, create the life you are in love with.

Once I made the decision to rise up and be the hero, my comeback story began. I sat down and took time to write out the life I wanted. What type of woman I wanted to become, what goals I wanted to accomplish, how I wanted my finances to look, what habits I wanted to implement into a lifestyle, what beliefs and values I would live by, and what mindset I would approach life with. After I wrote out the life I wanted to create, to be honest, I had an overwhelming feeling of "yeah, right!" Who was I kidding? I was living a life that I could barely breathe in; I could barely pay the bills. I could barely buy groceries. I had gained weight. I felt like no man I was attracted to would be attracted to me, and at this point, the only goal I had ever accomplished was graduating from college. I saw myself in such a setback situation; I didn't see how I could possibly make this comeback a reality. I was sitting in my home having a pity party about how this life would be lovely, but there is no way it would be a reality for me. Then a thought came into my mind: *If you don't start today, then when? If you don't start today, where will you be in one year, five years, ten years, or twenty years down the road? If you don't start today and you remain in the same place, what is worse? The pain of discipline it will take to get there, or the pain of regret and wondering what could have been if you had at least tried?*

My husband's aunt, JoAnn Barta, has an awesome quote that has stuck with me ever since I heard it. She says, "You are not born a winner or a loser; you are born a chooser." We all have the power to choose—the life we dream of, the life we commit to, and the life we are willing to fight for. What do you choose? I am so thankful that the fear of living a life haunted by regret for not even trying to achieve the life I dreamed of, shook me out of the cycle of inaction and allowed me to leverage that feeling of dread to move me into action. I started to shift from this mindset that the life I had written out on paper was someone else's life to owning that this is my life, whether it looks like it right now or not. I was not on a diet; it was my lifestyle. I was not working out to get in shape; it was my lifestyle. I did not live on a budget to pay off debt; it was my lifestyle. I chose the lifestyle that I wanted to live by. I chose the values that aligned with the lifestyle I wanted to create. I shifted my beliefs to align with the lifestyle my life would be marked by.

I would love to be able to say I rose up, I decided to make my comeback story a reality, and everything was happy-go-lucky. Well, my friends, guess what? That is not life, and that is definitely not the tale of a comeback story (or at least one that you want to hear). I had setbacks, I had hurdles, I had times I wanted to give up, and I definitely had to get up and choose to keep moving forward every single day. When something would come up, I had to decide: Will I allow this circumstance to make me a victim and dictate how my life is going to go, or will I rise up to be the hero and choose to live the life I want to live in spite of the circumstance coming my way? I can victoriously say I chose the hero route, BUT it wasn't easy. No matter the circumstances, I made sure to spend time with Jesus every day, and I knew that I had to keep my eyes fixed on Him. I had to keep my heart set on Him so I would not be distracted by anxiety, fear, or shame. Creating the discipline to cultivate a relationship with Jesus daily helped me remain at peace and make choices that were responsive and not reactive. When I had moments that I fell short, I would remind myself that every day is a new day; regardless of what happened yesterday, I get to choose again each and every day.

The key to a comeback is knowing that it will be beautifully imperfect. As a culture, we do not like imperfection. We search the world for perfection in everything, and we hold ourselves to live perfectly. When we don't live up to it, we get overwhelmed and disappointed, which causes us to throw in the towel. When you embrace imperfection and the reality that every day is a new day to choose, it creates a comeback culture in your life. Every day is a great day for your comeback story; you just have to choose it.

In my comeback story, I encountered Jesus. I cannot tell my story or talk about the changes in my life and my "comeback" without talking about Jesus. I am not here to convince anyone that Jesus is real and that He is their Lord and Savior. I am just here, sharing the full truth about my story as vulnerably as I can, and my story includes Jesus. Everyone is on their own spiritual journey, but I truly feel that if I don't share how Jesus impacted my journey, I will be doing a disservice to anyone who reads this chapter, and I would be ultimately dishonoring Jesus. In my story, I like to say that Jesus is the secret sauce! If I had not had my encounter with Him before all heck broke loose in my life, I know that I would not be where I am today or who I am today. Jesus has been my anchor in the midst of all of the storms and crazy circumstances. He has been my Jehovah Jireh, my provider when I was in need. He has been my peace through it all and my biggest cheerleader.

About two months before my rock-bottom moment, I had given my life to Jesus. I was so excited about this new relationship, and I was on fire for God. I couldn't wait to share my faith with my then-boyfriend, but after a week of him being home, he ended our relationship, a week before Christmas. The night it happened, I went to a friend's house, and I cried my eyes out to her. After I calmed down, she said she was going out to the bar with her boyfriend and asked if I wanted to come. I knew that if I went out, no good would come of it, so I chose to stay in her apartment alone. It was the longest night of my life. I don't think I slept at all.

The next day, I went to church, found my pastor, and cried my eyes out to him. I explained all that had happened the night before and asked him to pray for me. Thinking about that happening now makes me kind of chuckle; the poor pastor was probably beside himself that I was pouring my heart out as fast as I could in between services. He was very gracious, and he, of course, prayed for me.

After I left that church service, nothing was miraculously fixed; everything was still the same, but my heart felt a smidge of peace. I knew that no person could fix my situation or how I was feeling, but I knew that Jesus could. The fire for God I already had before now had kerosene poured on it. I was not going to run to people for help or comfort; I was going to run to Jesus, and that is exactly what I did. I would pray for hours and hours and hours every single day. I had pages of prayers I had written out that I would pray every single day. Every morning, I would wake up early and read His word and do a Bible study. I would practice fasting, whether it was coffee or food. I wanted to build a close, intimate relationship with God, and I was all in for Him. I did not want to miss a moment with Him. I was so serious about this that my mom stopped me one morning and said she was worried about me; she was worried I might commit suicide. I was able to tell her that I was not suicidal and that I was actually on my way to get baptized.

One of the first things I noticed after I started going all in with God was a change in my body. Before all of this had happened, I would have these very strange episodes of a stomachache that would make me keel over and not be able to stand up straight. Usually, to get it to go away, I would literally have to lie flat. I figured I had some sort of stomach ulcer, but I didn't want to know, so I never got it checked out. Once I was single and living all in, I realized I stopped having them. I was healed of whatever was causing me to have those awful stomachaches. To this day, I have never had another one.

In those days, I forged my relationship with God—I could hear His voice so clearly, and His peace guided me every single day. Whenever I saw my now ex call my phone, I would pray. I would pray that God would speak through me and that I wouldn't say the things I wanted to. I did this literally every time! I stayed strong and firm in the Lord, and He kept my peace constant. I was able to respond in kindness, even when he did not deserve it. I never broke or lashed out.

As time went on, Jesus continually remained faithful. He was the first man in my life who showed me what it means to be faithful.

When I gave my life to Jesus, I told Him, "Alright, if I am giving my life to You, I don't want to be like these Christians that say they believe in You, but you would never know it by the life they lead. I want to be marked by You, and I want my life to look like the life You have called me to live. I want a life marked by Your miracles. I want to be a disciple, not a mere Christian."

Let me tell you, He has held up His end of that conversation. I have seen so many miracles in my life. To some, they may not seem like miracles, but I know they are because without Jesus, they would never have happened. I won't share them all, but I will share a few of the big ones.

I have already shared the miracle of my stomach being healed, which has been amazing, but He has shown up in several different ways as well. When I was looking for a condo in Eagle, Idaho, it was a prime location. I did not want to live in a big complex; I wanted to live in these cute condos in the downtown area, but unfortunately, there were no vacancies. I decided I would check one last time before I gave up and looked at one of the bigger apartment complexes. When I went to check Craigslist, a new posting for a condo in the area I wanted was posted. I was able to go see it that same day. The landlord ended up being a Christian; he didn't make me do a credit check, and instead of collecting a deposit and first and last months' rent, he only required me to pay a deposit and first month's rent. He also gave it to me on the spot, and I ended up living there for over ten years!

When I decided I was going to go after being debt-free, the same day, my landlord sent me a text message saying he felt like the Holy Spirit was telling him not to cash my rent check, so he just wanted to let me know he was going to send it back to me. I was able to pay off my first student loan and part of another one with that money. I still have that check! One of the first Christmases I had with my daughter, I didn't have very much money for presents. In one week, I received two phone calls to come to the church because someone had dropped off a package for me. The first day, the package had new clothes for my daughter in it; the second day, the package had clothes for me, clothes for her, and an envelope. When I opened the envelope, there were several other envelopes, and each envelope I opened had cash in it. The cash ended up totaling $1,000; I had plenty to buy gifts and then some.

I will share one final story. I was in the survival era of my single mom journey. I had very few groceries—rice being our main staple—and I had $7 in the bank. I was frustrated and worried about food and finances. A friend invited me and my daughter over for Valentine's Day to have dinner with her and her husband. That evening, not only did we get a nice meal, but they dished up all of the leftovers and sent us home with them. On the way to the car, they also grabbed two huge paper grocery bags that were filled to the brim with groceries for us. I could go on and on with all of the miracles He has brought into my life, but I will leave it here. If any of these testimonies spoke to you, remember that God is not a respecter of persons; if He will do it for me, He will also do it for you. Testimony is literally translated as "do it again" in Hebrew, so every testimony we share, we are cheering God on to do it again!

All of the miracles are exciting and fun, but then it occurred to me: *What would it look like to live a life that didn't need God to bust in with His miracles?* I don't mean by playing it safe and not going for big things that do require God to show up for them to happen. I mean, what if I was living a life that I wasn't just trying to survive and always hanging on by a thread? What if I lived a life that I was actually living and not just surviving, so when God's miracles came through, it wasn't for food or bills being paid, it was for business deals or impacting the world somehow? When I was just surviving life, I was living in the moment of each day, not having the energy to think proactively and disrupt the cycle I was on to change the trajectory of my life. I wasn't able to live in the fullest expression of who I am designed to be. I was stifled, cut off at the throat, and held hostage by my own life circumstances. When I decided to draw the line in the sand and stop allowing life circumstances to control my life and instead live the life I was destined for anyhow, it was a game-changer. How did I create the change? One choice at a time, toward one goal at a time, aligned with God.

I clearly remember when I had this thought go through my mind: *If I don't change something today, when will I change? If I don't start moving forward toward my goals in life, will I still be in the same place, however many years down the road? If I don't change, will I always be in this same place of barely surviving life and always dreaming and wishing about the future? What if the future I am dreaming about never comes?* All of these thoughts came to me at once, and I knew I could not wait a second longer. I had to change, and I had to change now. If you asked yourself those questions, how would you answer? Have you found yourself constantly in preparation mode that turns into procrastination that then paralyzes you and keeps you from actually taking action? Have you found yourself getting everything just right, starting to take action, but then something in life comes up to derail you, so you just throw in the towel and say, "Well, I tried," or "Maybe next year," or "It's just not meant to be"? If so, I hear you, and I feel you, but it does not have to be this way! You can change the pattern and cycle you have known to a new pattern and cycle that gets you results every time. I know, because I have done it, over and over again!

When we think about goals, what is one of the top things people say you must have to reach a goal? Common answers would be motivation, willpower, and drive. I think these are all great things to help you get there, but they are not what your results are relying on. Motivation comes and goes, willpower will only take you so far, and drive without direction can take you in circles. You have to create a lifestyle that says completing your goals is part of who you are; it is etched into your identity. There is no room for negotiating with yourself; you can no longer put it off until tomorrow. The action you must take to reach your goals must happen, and you get to do it because it is a part of who you are. You must choose every day, regardless of how you feel. Do you feel like you want to go to work every day? No, but you do it, or you get fired. Do you feel like filling your car up with gas every time? No, but you do, or you will run out and not be able to go anywhere. Do you feel like paying your car payment? No, but you do so that your car isn't repossessed. I say all of that to make the point that, for some reason, we have attached taking action toward our goals with emotion, with feeling, and that is setting you up for failure.

If I had taken action only when I felt like it, I would have never achieved any of my goals. We must create a non-emotional discipline, drive, and hunger to reach our goals. It must be a "must" in our lives, not a "would be nice." When I shifted my mindset to accepting that taking action toward my goals is who I am and what I do, I stopped negotiating with myself when I would take action; I just did it. I would get home from a long day at work, coaching softball—dirty, sweaty, and tired—but I would automatically turn on my workout and get started before I sat down. I would be hungry and crave something unhealthy, but I would reach for already-prepped foods that were aligned with my lifestyle because I knew the taste would never be as satisfying as the feeling of accomplishing my goals and feeling good in my clothes. I would go to donate plasma, not because I wanted a huge, fat needle stuck in my arm, but because I was a woman determined to be debt-free, and that was going to get me one step closer. I changed the way I would go grocery shopping. I changed the way I spent money. I changed the way I invested my time to align with the lifestyle of achieving my goals, and I would bring my goals before God in my prayer time. This shift led to me reaching all of my goals—not just some—all of them.

As I started reaching my goals, each goal I reached served as a stepping stone that led to the next. Momentum was created by every small win, each decision that was made in alignment with the lifestyle of reaching my goal. I did not reach my goals by making a few aligned decisions and then a month later, or 60 days, or even 90 days later, I reached my goal. I had to show up each and every day for a year, and sometimes multiple years, to finally reach and achieve my goal. The length of time differed depending on which one I was after, but not one was reached in less than a year. I find that so many people have given up on their goals, or don't even try, because they feel it happens for everyone else but not for them. They think *I am so far behind, why even start?* Or they get caught up in comparison with everyone else's highlight reels on social media, so they are too embarrassed to start. A huge tip for starting off on creating a new lifestyle to achieve your goals: Tune out the distractions—and I mean specifically—tune out social media. If it doesn't serve you, it is more than likely stealing from you! Do not allow social media to steal the wind from your sails as you embark on this new journey. Unfortunately, so many people are not being fully transparent or fabricating their stories to make it look like they reached their goals overnight. On rare occasions, one of those stories might be true, but most of them are not.

Social media will burn you, so if you are going to continue using it, discipline yourself to stay away from stories or people that make you feel bad about yourself or make you feel negative; that is stealing from you, not serving you.

I was a single mom for twelve years while I achieved all of these goals, but that doesn't mean I went through it alone. I had several mentors and coaches in my life. I consider God, Jesus, and the Holy Spirit my primary mentors, but I also had several people who showed up in my life to help me. I had a friend who was about ten years older than me, and she was my biggest mentor; she took me through the deep-dive moments into the depths of my past, my identity, my limiting beliefs, my false beliefs, generational curses, and so much more. She truly helped me lay the foundation of who I am and who I am still becoming. I had another friend, who is about thirty years older, who mentored me in raising my daughter, handling conflict, and dating. I had my mom and cousin, who helped me as accountability partners to work out and eat healthy every day. I have had so many mentors speaking into my life and coaching me along my journey; I can confidently say that without all of them, I don't think I would be where I am or who I am.

Now, let's take a moment to think about professional athletes. How many athletes do you think have made it to the professional level without a coach or a mentor? Do you think Tiger Woods, Michael Jordan, Mia Hamm, or Lisa Leslie made it to the level of their career they did by going solo? Not one of them! It is interesting that we can see how it only makes sense for those people to have coaches, but when we are trying to reach our own goals as a "normal person," we think it is unnecessary to have a coach. A coach is someone who comes alongside us and not only encourages us to continue on the path but also has the invitation to call out our blind spots, call us up to a better level, help us implement strategy, and hone our skills. A coach is the person who is supposed to draw the gold out of us and help refine us so that not only do we reach our goals, but we are still whole when we arrive. They provide you with the motivation, inspiration, and structure to keep your fire burning in the right direction without burnout. A coach isn't only necessary in sports, athletics, and fitness; we need them in business, parenting, finance, and our spiritual relationship, to name a few. These people may not all be referred to as a coach specifically; you may refer to them as a mentor or something else, but they stand in the same space.

Personally, I have coached so many different people at so many different ages. I remember when I was in high school, I helped coach the goalies of a young girls' soccer team. In college, I was the head coach of my younger sister's youth basketball team. As a mom, I was an assistant coach of my daughter's club softball team. In my career, I was the office manager and then the COO for a total of ten years. In those ten years, I spent most of my time coaching people, mainly women, on how to communicate through conflict or just how to communicate in general. In the gym, I was a group exercise instructor, coaching groups of men and women through lifting weights or high-impact cardio workouts. In my faith, I helped lead women through faith-based group exercise classes, I taught 5- and 6-year-olds all about Jesus, and I helped troubled teens see their identity in Jesus. My life has been truly marked by coaching, whether you are looking at it from a receiving or giving standpoint. I am still, to this day, being coached and coaching others. In June 2024, I started my official coaching business for women to help them connect with God to achieve their goals, and in July, I hired a business coach to help me create the business of my dreams.

Coaching is amazing, but it doesn't do the work for me. I still have to show up and put in the work. This goes back to planning and preparing: If all I do is talk about what I need to do in my business, but I never actually take action, then it doesn't matter how much coaching I receive; I will never get to my goal. All the G.O.A.T.s out there—Tony Robbins, Simone Biles, Warren Buffett, and Henry Ford, to name a few—had coaches and mentors. I want to highlight that coaches and mentors are plural—they had more than one. It is pretty outrageous to think these amazing people all needed coaches, but we don't believe we need a coach in life. Stop deceiving yourself and find a coach, or several of them! If you want to see lasting change in your life and you want to achieve what matters most to you, stop negotiating with yourself; find a coach who can get you results and start to take action!

The final message I want you to leave with is this: Watch your mouth! By that, I mean, watch what words you allow out of it. I don't know if you have heard this before, but our words have the power of life or death when we speak; we choose which one we are projecting over whatever we are talking about. There is no in-between! Let me give you some evidence outside of my words to back this up.

If you're a Christian, the Bible clearly states in Proverbs 18:21, *"Death and life are in the power of the tongue, and those who love it will eat of its fruit."* The first half of this verse, *"Death and life are in the power of the tongue,"* offers a bold truth: Every word we speak is either planting seeds of life or seeds of death. There's no neutral ground. This simple but profound principle has the power to radically shift the trajectory of your life.

Take a moment and consider some of the "innocent" yet life-shaping phrases we say without a second thought. When I began to confront this truth and take inventory of my own words, I realized I was regularly saying things like, "I'm broke," "I can't afford that," "My job sucks the life out of me," "You're killing me," and "I'm too tired." These may seem harmless—just exaggerations, expressions, or jokes—but our words don't lose power because we don't mean them seriously. Whether intentional or casual, our words are always sowing something—either life or death.

The second part of that verse, *"and those who love it will eat of its fruit,"* reflects the biblical law of sowing and reaping. Whatever you consistently speak, believe, and act on, you will eventually harvest. Your words are seeds, and the fruit will show up, whether it's sweet or bitter.

I experienced this firsthand during one of the hardest seasons of my life. I was a single mom with over $25,000 in debt, receiving no child support, but I had a deep conviction: I wanted to be debt-free before I got married. Even when my reality didn't align with that dream, I chose to speak faith. I would thank Jesus in advance for my debt being paid in full, even though I still had a long way to go. Sometimes life made it feel like I was moving backward, but I kept declaring the same thing. For nearly ten years, I sowed words of faith, belief, and action—until I finally saw the breakthrough. My debt was fully paid off. About nine months later, I met my now husband.

Your words are creating your reality—so if you don't like what you see, start changing what you say.

If you are into science, Dr. Masaru Emoto, a Japanese scientist, performed an experiment where two different jars of water were subjected to two different types of words. One jar was subjected to positive words, and the other was exposed to negative words. He froze the water and placed samples under a microscope. The water that was exposed to positive words formed beautiful crystals, while the water subjected to negative words formed irregular shapes or no shape at all. How much of the human body is made of water? Men are about 60 percent water, women are about 55 percent water, young children are about 65 percent, and infants are about 75 percent water. If we are subjecting ourselves to positive words, how do you think that might impact our bodies, knowing the results of this experiment? Now, think of the impact negative words might have on our bodies. I don't know about you, but I want my body's water composition to be made up of beautiful crystals, not rendered formless or into irregular shapes. You can also find evidence about how rice changes in a very similar experiment; the positive jar of rice stays white with some yellow, whereas the negative jar becomes moldy and brown. Your words matter, and if you don't believe me, Google it!

In Dr. Emoto's research, he also experimented with written words, music, and thoughts. With thought, all of his findings performed the same way as if the words were spoken. So I want to take this a step further: What are you consuming? What are you believing? What are you imagining? Our outer world matters, but so does our inner world!

Let's start with beliefs: Our lives hinge on our beliefs, our identity is built upon our beliefs, and who we become is the expression of our beliefs. If our beliefs are positive, empowering, and in alignment with the vision we have for our lives, we are unstoppable as long as we don't quit. If our beliefs are laced with lies and doubts and in conflict with the vision we have for our lives, they will be the silent dream-killers, self-sabotaging you every single time. It is important to sit down and evaluate what you believe. Where did your beliefs come from? Did they come from your parents, peers, teachers, coaches, or past experiences? It is interesting how we can become adults and attempt to live the life of our dreams, but most of us have never taken the time to really understand why we believe what we believe, to see if those beliefs are worth holding onto or if they need to be traded in for better ones. If you want to experience a true breakthrough in your life, pay attention right now. If there is one thing out of this chapter I want you to hear, it's this: Do a deep dive into your beliefs, discover what limiting beliefs you are holding onto, and annihilate them. You do not have precious time to waste carrying around limiting beliefs that are silently stopping you from living in the fullness of your identity and design.

You may be thinking, *"Well, that is easy for you to say, but how am I supposed to do that?!"* Well, it is easy! Take inventory of all of your beliefs—positive and negative. If a belief is positive and empowering, keep it. If a belief is negative, insecure, or possibly toxic, it's time to trade it in. The funny thing is, usually the limiting belief, when reversed, is the empowering belief you need. For example, I have struggled with a limiting belief that I was too much or not enough. It is a very frustrating place to be when the limiting belief goes both ways! The empowering belief that I traded that limiting belief in for is, *I am more than enough! I am never too much, and I am never not enough! I am the daughter of God, and He has made me more than enough!* This belief, all on its own, has been liberating for me.

It is also wise to take note of where your limiting beliefs started. Did that belief originate from a parent, a counselor, a coach, or a friend? If it originally came from an outside source, it is time to take away the power of that voice and redirect that power to your own voice. You get to say who you are or who you are not; you get to say what beliefs you will build your life on. No matter where it originated, if it was negative, it is time to trade it in and declare it is wrong. Once you have your limiting beliefs rewritten, it's time to take action! We are going to declare out loud who you are and what you no longer have room to hold onto in your life. Stand up, go look yourself square in the mirror, and start declaring, "I no longer believe (state limiting belief); it has no power over my life as of right now! I believe (state empowering belief), this is who I am, and this is who I will become!" Do this for every single one, and turn this into a daily practice until you start to feel the shift in your demeanor, in your day-to-day energy, and in the way you approach life. I still do this to this day. It's not every day, but when I need a boost, I get in the mirror and get in my face! Remember: Your beliefs dictate your life, so take the time and rewrite your story!

Besides Jesus, our beliefs are the foundation we build our lives upon, but even if we have our empowered beliefs and our relationship with Jesus, if we are speaking death left and right, we are still self-sabotaging. As we talked about earlier, our words matter; they will either speak life or death—there is no in-between, so what do you choose? The words that follow an "I am" statement should be held close to you because they will become your own self-fulfilling prophecy. I want to encourage you to be intentional about every word that you allow out of your mouth. You will either be creating the amazing future you are dreaming about or creating a world filled with disappointment and doubt. Which one would you prefer? I, for one, choose to create a life of a self-fulfilling prophecy of success. I hope you choose that too. Don't allow your mouth, your voice, or your words to tear down all the work you have created with the massive action you have been taking. Your actions and your words must be in alignment and must work together; otherwise, you will just be constantly working against yourself, causing you to stay stuck or, worse, to quit!

When you start to speak positivity into your life, dreams, and passions, what would have been a setback will be turned into an opportunity. Opportunities will allow you to learn and pivot, imperfectly pressing forward to create progress and ultimately momentum. Disrupt the pattern you have seen before, take hold of your words and beliefs, align them with truth and your vision to empower you to fulfill your dreams and achieve success.

To summarize everything we have talked about in this chapter, it is never too late to start your comeback story; you just have to rise up and decide to be the hero of your own story. You must have a spiritual connection, and in my opinion, Jesus is the secret sauce. He came in and did the heavy lifting for you; now you just have to follow through and take action. Choose to be disciplined and stop negotiating; each choice made in alignment with your goals creates the momentum you need to achieve your goals. The best in the world have coaches; who are we to think we don't need a coach to master life? Our beliefs dictate our reality, and our words either bring our dreams into reality or tear them apart. If your beliefs don't align with the truth and who you want to become, all you have to do is choose new ones to rewrite your story. Once you are aligned with your vision and your beliefs are in check, speak life! Shout it from the rooftops! Partner your words with your vision so you get there faster, and you eliminate that old pattern of self-sabotage, allowing yourself to finally create lasting change!

Thank you for sticking with me this long and reading my story. I hope reading this gives you hope that if I can achieve all that I have, so can you! I hope that you have a fire within you to rise up and start your comeback story today, right now. It is your time. Don't put it off for another year, month, week, day, or hour. The time is now, and you can do it! The hero you have been waiting for is you. It's time to rise up and go for it. If you don't know Jesus, He is just waiting for you to call on His name and accept Him as your Lord and Savior. If you want to chat more about who Jesus is before you are ready to accept Him into your life, feel free to reach out to me, and let's connect! The life you have been waiting for is literally just one choice away; what do you choose? I hope you choose you! If you are ready and excited to finally reach your goals and create the lasting change you have been burning for, and you recognize that you not only need a coach but you want a coach, let's do this thing! I work with women like you and me to help them connect with God to achieve their goals and not sacrifice what matters most to them. If you are a mama, you can be the supermom you are striving to be and achieve your goals and dreams as well, without the mom guilt. I am out here doing it every day, and so can you! Ladies, it's time to step into the fullness of who you are created and destined to be! We don't have time to mess around; time is precious, and it's not slowing down. Let's do this together and do it now. Don't let another day go by the same as yesterday; take action, get results, and live a life that roars louder than your voice ever could.

Kelley Weinzetl is a Christian Coach with over 10 years of experience helping women grow, heal, and step into lasting transformation. In June 2024, she launched *Dare 2 Roar*—a coaching movement created to help high-achieving women reconnect with God and partner with Him to pursue their purpose without sacrificing what matters most.

She lives in Eagle, Idaho, with her husband of two years and their two children. When she's not coaching, you can find her working out, indulging in chocolate and peanut butter, or dancing around the kitchen in worship with her family.

Kelley would love to hear from you! Mention that you read this book to receive an exclusive discount on your coaching package.

∼

To connect with Kelley:
—
Email: kelley@dare2roar.com
—
Instagram: @Dare_2_Roar.

FROM CRISIS TO CUSTODIAN: THE RISE OF A WARRIOR WOMAN

BY NADIA JACOBS

She is a wife, a mother, a businesswoman, and a warrior. A woman who has danced with success and stared down unimaginable hardship, yet never lost her fire. She built her life from the ground up. She led in male-dominated industries, raised a family, and faced the kind of financial collapse that would bring most to their knees. But she didn't break. She rebuilt—with grit, with purpose, and with an unstoppable spirit that refused to surrender.

She wrote this chapter as a testament for those walking a path that feels unbearable. For the ones silently carrying the weight of the world. For the women and men who hold their families together while feeling like they're falling apart. For those wanting to have a better life. For those wanting to open new doors with a determined mindset and an unstoppable spirit.

She's lived it. She's been in the trenches repeatedly. She's made money, lost it, rebuilt it, and redefined what freedom means. She doesn't speak from theory; she speaks from experience. She's proof that even when the system breaks you, and you're crawling through the storm, you can walk out of it and rebuild beyond it. And that's exactly why she's here now—not just to share her story, but to light the way forward.

During the global pandemic, she discovered a new path out of the ashes of chaos. A path toward a sense of freedom that doesn't ask for permission. One grounded in self-leadership, purpose, drive, and truth.

Her mission was always bigger than survival. It was about education. About giving back and helping others reclaim a power they never knew they had. She wanted to show people that there were many ways—smarter ways, clearer ways—to step outside the box.

And for those quietly wondering where their journey might begin, the question was gentle but undeniable: **Are you ready to be part of something more?** Are you ready to learn how to turn pain into purpose, fear into fuel, and breakdowns into breakthroughs?

Her hope is simple but powerful:

- That after reading this, women and men everywhere remember the unstoppable force they truly are.
- That they awaken the warrior within.
- That they realize they are never truly alone.
- That they reject mediocrity and step into a bold new future—as independent beings, as conscious investors, as critical thinkers, and as freedom warriors, not worriers.
- That they don't just dream of freedom and change but take the leap and align with the caliber of people who will empower them into a future they own.

WHEN THE WORLD FORGOT HER, SHE REMEMBERED HERSELF

There's a quiet kind of suffering most will never understand—the kind where a woman fights battles no one else sees. Where she cries in the shower, breathes through the pain, and then walks out smiling, with her head up and her big-girl pants on, because her family needs her and everyone is relying on her. That was her. A warrior in disguise. A lioness cloaked in silk.

She wasn't building the life others expected of her—not the one indoctrinated by society, where you trade your time, your energy, and your soul just to pay off debt and call it security. That life felt suffocating. She was done surviving. She was building the life she truly wanted—one that was free, aligned with her values, and worth waking up for. One that gave her choices and freedom.

HER JOURNEY TO BECOMING UNSTOPPABLE

Her journey began in the beauty industry, where she worked as an employee, trading her time for money for fourteen years. Building someone else's dreams rather than her own. Deep down, something in her spirit screamed for more—she knew she wanted to run her own company one day. She transitioned into a subcontractor role as a beauty therapist. The moment she stepped into that role, she made more money than ever, and the fog lifted. It was her first taste of real freedom to create the life she desired, and it was intoxicating.

From that point on, everything changed. Working half the hours as a subcontractor and earning triple the income, she had a revelation: She knew then she was capable of anything she set her mind to. The idea of running her own company no longer felt distant. With the right mindset and persistent drive, she saw it clearly: She wasn't just capable of building a company—she was born to build an empire.

Later, she took on a high-pressure role as an Incident Report Manager for one of Australia's leading organizations. She became the central point of contact for all critical incidents across statewide retail stores from the late hours of the evening to the morning sunrise. Her responsibility was to remain calm, find solutions, and maintain order during the most chaotic moments. She didn't fold—*she rose*. She learned how to lead in the fire. How to think fast. How to deliver when it mattered most.

Her combined experiences as an employee, entrepreneur, and subcontractor sparked a deeper desire for even more. In 2009, she stepped into an entrepreneurial role and quickly earned her first six figures—sharing nutraceutical products, building global teams, and running events. She traveled overseas, gave back to communities, and played a key part in building a strong community online and offline with like-minded people. From that moment on, working for someone else was no longer an option. She had tasted freedom—and there was no going back.

Together, she and her husband made a decision to build something of their own—something that aligned not just with their goals but with their values, their vision, and their purpose. She would not only own her company but also expand it, carving her path as a leader in entrepreneurship and scaling her vision with purpose.

In 2011, she became a registered business owner as a licensed Private Investigator (P.I.) and began operating as a self-employed subcontractor in the private investigations and security field. Despite her consistent efforts to obtain work and gain contacts within the industry, she faced constant rejection. Every company she contacted shut her down—every email, every resume, every phone call was met with coldness, arrogance, and dismissive responses. She felt like she was a nobody, and her spirit started to break. The thought of giving up even crossed her mind.

Imagine trying to establish a name in an industry where no one will give you a chance. She was made to feel invisible—like she didn't belong. But rather than accepting defeat, her response was simple: "If no one will give me a shot, I'll create my own path." That moment became her defining catalyst. She wasn't just going to prove them wrong—she was going to build something that could never be dismissed. With her husband by her side, they built everything from the ground up—bootstrapped, self-funded, and backed by pure heart and soul.

She entered a male-dominated industry with confidence and class as a newly registered private investigations and security company. With no outside funding or support—just a clear vision, a determined spirit, and a powerful drive to lead. As CEO, she navigated this world with authority and with precision, grace, and fire rather than aggression. She had heart and class all wrapped in one, which drove clients to want to book with her. Every call, every email. All the accounts, all the jobs she took on—she did it all with her soft yet firm voice. Clients didn't just seek her assistance; they sought her guidance, her wisdom, and her ability to provide clarity and solutions.

She soon became well-known in the industry and realized that in a field where women were rare, she was exactly what people wanted: a caring yet solid woman who not only understood her position but also delivered intelligent, clear, and confident responses that brought results. But few knew the true depth of her sacrifice, her consistent work to build something that could never be taken away.

As the company grew, so did their family. With three beautiful children and a devoted, supportive husband, life began to reflect the vision she had always held in her heart. They built their first home together.

Her husband often said she was the woman who wore many hats and shoes and was a natural at pivoting with grace and grit. He was her rock and anchor—the one who always encouraged her to grow into the woman she was destined to be: limitless, fierce, and unstoppable.

And she was his peace, his world, his heart.

Three children. A thriving business. A hand-built property. A life many admired. She was internally grateful and happy. She went off to buy her second property, then her third. Life was good. She was exactly where she was meant to be. Hardworking and honest, she achieved everything she had always craved.

But she didn't see the war she was about to endure.

WHEN THE GLOBAL PANDEMIC STOLE THE GROUND BENEATH HER

The world health crisis hit like a hurricane and shut down her investigation and security company. Everything collapsed at once. Contracts vanished. The phone stopped ringing. Income disappeared overnight. But the bills kept coming. For the first time in a long time, she was no longer in control.

She burned through savings. Ate less so her kids could eat more. She borrowed from her children's piggy banks and whispered promises to pay it back. Most nights, she cried after her children went to bed—not just from exhaustion, but from guilt. Guilt for the many years of working too hard and taking on extra roles. For not having an emergency backup plan to keep the family afloat in unexpected times. Guilt for no longer being the version of herself they once knew. She became a shell of herself, unable to make sense of what was happening. She had lost everything—including herself.

Scraping together money became a desperate game in the house—she'd get all her kids to play "Let's find any money in the house," digging through drawers, cupboards, old purses, piggy banks, and tins—anything that might hold a forgotten coin—just to afford a loaf of bread.

She was brought to her knees in prayer, the weight of everything pressing down on her chest. She begged for a miracle—not for riches, but for **relief**. She asked the universe, God, anyone who would listen, to help her hold on to all that she and her husband had built... But the mountain of debt now loomed like a storm.

Two hundred thousand dollars of property debt and bills continuously piling up with no break sat like a chain around her ankles, tethering her to a financial system that no longer made sense. She wasn't praying for wealth. She was praying to breathe. For a way to protect her family. For a way to feel alive again. Yet, a quiet, defiant voice inside kept whispering: *You will not fall. You've come too far to give up now.*

She hid her pain well and still showed up! She got up. She faced another day. Alone. Silent. Fighting. Unseen. She had lost her way. She questioned everything—*Why am I here? What is happening? Do I even exist?*

And then the day came. She could no longer hold off on the mortgages or stretch the money to cover expenses. She made a decision.

SOMETHING HAD TO CHANGE

As the bills continued to pile up, she made the call—an executive decision made from desperation and fear, not choice. If she didn't act now, she and her family could lose everything they had built together. Her hands trembled. Her heart pounded. Tears streamed down her face as she waited two hours on hold with the bank.

When the call was finally answered, her voice cracked before it even formed words. She broke down. She sobbed out loud, hoping that if they could just *hear* her pain and *feel* the sorrow in her voice, they'd offer grace. Just a sliver of leniency.

"I don't have any money," she pleaded. "Just give me some time."

"Please... I didn't choose this. Everything is shut down. The whole world is suffering. We are suffering. I've spent my life building everything, and now I can't even earn enough to feed my children, let alone pay the mortgages. I'm not trying to escape this—I'm just trying to survive. I'm not lazy. I'm not running. I'm begging you for time."

Silence. Then, the banker's voice returned, flat as concrete. "Miss, you're one of hundreds of thousands."

That was it. She was a number. Another desperate voice swallowed by a system that didn't care. No humanity. No grace. No choice. The only option he gave was sink or drown: a six-month freeze. No payments. No help. Just interest quietly compounding, like poison in the dark. And she accepted. Not because it was fair or because it would save her. Because she had no other choice, she was tied to the system.

The banker asked her to repeat her name and say yes on the recorded line. And within minutes, it was done.

She hung up the phone and cried; then she stood up and danced. A raw, defiant, barefoot-in-the-kitchen kind of celebratory dance not born of hope, but of *desperate relief*. For just one breath in time, she wasn't drowning. A tiny victory. She was still in the fight. She was vulnerable but still sharp and already calculating her next move.

She negotiated a freeze across all three properties. Six months. No payments. No support from the bank—just a freeze. No government handouts, no business relief. As a private investigator she knew how to track people, so she also knew how to disappear so no one could ever track her. But that invisibility came at a cost: The government couldn't verify her or her business. And that meant no help.

She was completely on her own, but it felt like she could breathe for the first time again. She knew after the call she would have enough time to get back on her feet, now that all mortgages were paused for six months.

THE CALM BEFORE THE COLLAPSE

Six months passed—quickly, quietly. During that time, she focused on her children, fully immersed in homeschooling, pouring herself into their little minds while holding hers together with faith and hope.

Every day, she whispered the same prayer: *God, please help us. Let me restart. Let me rebuild. Let me bring my family back from this hardship and rise above it.* She believed, with everything in her, that soon she could return to the company, get things back on track, and recover what had been lost.

And why wouldn't she believe that? The bank was there to help everyone, right? That's what she thought. Until the phone rang exactly six months later. There was no warmth in the voice that greeted her—only scripted lines, sterile and sharp, like a blade dressed in politeness.

The voice that came through didn't see a woman holding her family together by a thread. It saw a number. A problem to be resolved. A name to cross off the list. They confirmed her identity like a criminal check. Date of birth. Address. Loan reference number. Then, flatly:

"So, how's that money coming along to start paying the mortgages?"

Her chest tightened.

"Mrs. Jacobs, it's time to start paying." She blinked, stunned, and stared into nothingness as if she were frozen in time.

"Mrs Jacobs... Are you still there?"

Her throat tightened. She swallowed hard. "How much?" she finally whispered, her voice crackling, as her heart sank in despair, knowing she still could not pay the mortgage. She was still unable to work. No one could work—she was still in a lockdown state with no idea when it would all end.

And just like that, the banker confidently stated, "Your new monthly repayments are now $7800 a month. Can you confirm you can start paying this as of next month to get things back on track?"

Her stomach twisted. A cold wave surged through her. She gripped the edge of the counter like it was the only thing keeping her upright. Something broke. Not loud. Not angry. Just quiet devastation—the kind that creeps in when you realize *you might actually lose everything.*

She finally spoke, in a quiet, lifeless voice: "But... it used to be $1200 a month."

There was no reaction. Just silence. Cold. Then came the hammer.

"Mrs. Jacobs, I'm sorry to inform you," he said, "but that repayment no longer exists. That was before *you* chose to stop paying your mortgage and freeze the accounts. Your total debt is now **$1.70 million**, with monthly repayments of **$7800 interest-only repayments.** Would you like to pay the principal on top of that, Mrs. Jacobs?"

She blinked, heart hammering against her ribs. "What do you mean?" she whispered. "How can that be? The mortgage was only $200,000... You must have the wrong person. This—this can't be right." But the voice didn't waver.

"No, Mrs. Jacobs. We have the correct file. You're now responsible for the full amount. Do you have a payment method ready?"

Broken, she asked, "How?"

"Simple," they replied. "The interest kept compounding on the mortgages. You would have heard that in the disclaimer when you agreed to the freeze…"

She must have missed that part about the interest compounding on all three properties. The phone slipped from her hand. Her knees buckled. She collapsed on the cold kitchen floor. The room spun. She was unraveling. For a moment, she believed it was all over. This was the end of everything.

Her brain spinning out of control—head racing at the very thought of how she had been working most of her life alongside her husband, giving everything she could so her family could have the best life, only to be stripped bare of everything—and told she now owed it back, five times over.

THE COLLAPSE: $1.70 MILLION

She wept. For the years she'd built, her time, her effort—all she had carried and created with her husband and children. For the home she might lose. For the dreams that seemed to vanish in one cruel moment. But even as she sobbed on the kitchen floor, she was already rising inside; she just didn't know it yet. She could feel herself hanging by a thread, one tug away from losing it all. Her husband heard her tears of pain and went in and knelt beside her, speaking softly, "Please stop crying … You are crying so much… Where has the warrior inside you gone—the go-getter, the one that never gives up?"

Through tears of anguish and exhaustion, she cried out in frustration. Her prayers had gone unanswered. She had begged for a miracle, and nothing had come. She sobbed, confessing how she had used every last coin from her children's piggy banks—all their bank savings—believing with all her heart that God would rescue them through a lottery win that she had been praying for. She had truly believed she'd be the one. The one God would save to win. That faith would reward her. That she'd be the miracle story.

Her husband gently wiped the tears from her face, then rested his hand on her heart as he spoke softly, "You've been playing the lottery and praying to win… But what did you expect to happen? Why would you win over the millions of others begging for a miracle? Maybe you're praying for the wrong thing. Maybe it's time to ask for something different. Maybe it's time to stop crying and become the woman you were born to be."

Then he pulled her in close and wrapped his arms around her, holding her tight. His voice was soft but steady as he whispered words of encouragement. Then, rising to his feet, he said, "You are an amazing, beautiful, soulful woman who's done more, carried more, and given more than anyone I know. And there's already so much to be thankful for. We have to be grateful for what we do have. Who cares if we lose everything? We have each other."

She stared at him, stunned. "What do you mean, who cares?" she snapped. "I care."

And for a moment, she thought a punch to his forehead might feel strangely satisfying—*if only she had the strength,* she thought.

But something shifted... With a fierce look on her face, she stood up. Fire in her eyes. Then, with a firm, bold voice, she said, "No. I'm going to find another prayer. Another way. There's no way I'm letting them win. No way they're taking everything I've poured my soul into and fought so hard for. This is my 'take back what's mine moment.'"

And there she was—a lioness, redressing herself in her armor. She wiped her tears, slowly and deliberately, as if lining her face with war paint —ready to go to battle. Solid in her stance, she straightened her crown and said,

"They tried to break me.

"They forgot I was born for this.

"You are right," she said to her husband.

"It's time to be the woman I was born to be."

Her voice was calm. Because this wasn't just survival anymore. This was the rise.

Her husband stood there quietly for a moment—head tilted, pride softening his expression as he took in her strength, her grace under fire, her grit—he smiled and whispered, "There she is. There's my woman."

She knew there and then—some pain does not destroy. It *activates*. And sometimes, the only way to glory is straight through the fire. Because warriors don't wait for rescue—they fight, barefoot and bloody, until they win.

In the quiet that followed, she reached out to a trusted friend—

someone who had seen her strength long before she could see it again herself. She poured out everything. The fear. The guilt. And without hesitation, her friend looked her dead in the eye and said, "You're too smart to stay stuck. Get up. Find a way to become debt-free. Financially free. Independent. Fast."

She didn't ask for a hero. She became one. She didn't just survive. She awakened. She didn't wait for someone to save her. She saved herself. She didn't become a victim. She became a victor. She decided then and there: Never again would she let a broken system define her worth. She stopped playing by other people's rules and started writing her own.

She started to pray again—only this time, she prayed for direction. For clarity. For alignment with the path she was meant to walk. This time, she asked for the right people. The right opportunities. The right lifeline to help her rise, to take her on a journey onto a new pathway.

She was open and ready.

And then—just as she asked—a door cracked open. She knew she had to put action into her prayers. She immersed herself in studying how to become debt-free and break free from financial chains. She strategized how to become unbanked and decentralized on the blockchain. She joined online communities in the blockchain space, aligned with people who shared her vision for true freedom and custodianship.

Then an opportunity came like a knock at the door. A new online business presented itself. She looked at the person offering it and said, "You could be offering me a bag of potatoes right now, and I would still say yes." This was her lifeline, her prayer answered, and she wasn't missing it. She grabbed it with both hands.

A week went by. Doubt crept in. That old familiar voice—what if this doesn't work? What if I fail again? What if this is too good to be true? Weeks went by, and she held back out of fear that it wouldn't work. Then, after four weeks of overthinking with no changes, she realized the mind was a battlefield and she had to conquer that fear. She remembered who she was and moved forward with purpose, taking on that opportunity even if it did seem like a bag of potatoes.

Before she began, she sat on the lounge room floor and told her father what she was about to do. With passion in her voice and vision in her heart, she explained that she was going to build something big. Something that could shift lives. But instead of support, she was met with a wall.

"Stop being stupid," he said flatly. "Get back to work. That's not real life."

The words landed like cold steel—but instead of silencing her, they stirred something deeper.

He wasn't the only one. Others laughed. They doubted her and said she was dreaming too big, reaching too far. But every smirk, every whisper, and every eye-roll only pushed her harder. It didn't weaken her; it fueled her. She became more focused. More determined to prove that their limitations didn't belong to her.

Within six months, she didn't just rise—she transformed into an entrepreneur in the online space. She built one of the fastest-growing, most dynamic multi-level marketing organizations of her time, reaching top-tier status with an unstoppable force. But what most people never saw was the fire behind it—the reason she moved the way she did.

She reclaimed her power. She didn't just survive. She found her purpose: to guide others to freedom. To show them that there was another way. She became a light in the decentralized space—someone who had been broken, tested, laughed at, and underestimated—and who turned every single hardship into fuel. Every brick thrown her way? She used it to build her fortress. Her legacy. Her empire. She didn't just build wealth. She built *freedom*. She built *legacy*. She built *herself*.

ONE POINT SEVENTY MILLION REASONS TO RISE

Then came March 2022. She finally became debt-free and independent. One of the most extraordinary and elusive breakthroughs in modern life—a level of liberation most people chase for decades, yet never grasp.

But she did it. Together with her husband, they paid off **$1.70 million** in debt. Let that sink in. Not credit cards. Not small loans. A full-blown one-point-seventy-million-dollar mountain of pressure, stress, and sacrifice—**obliterated**. No handouts. No inheritance. No shortcuts. With sheer determination, strategy, grit, and grace, they did it.

This was more than a miracle. For the first time in her adult life, she could breathe. Stand tall. Walk freely. She didn't owe a soul. She had reclaimed power in its rawest, most sacred form: **ownership**.

And just when it should have been time to celebrate... in the blink of an eye, the ground beneath her gave way again. The company she built and grew that paid off that heavy burden collapsed within weeks of celebrating her freedom.

All of it gone. Not a dollar left to celebrate. No reward. No glory. She had crossed the finish line, and the bridge burned behind her. But even then, even in the ashes, she knew one thing: The foundation had been laid. Something greater was waking up. The real empire hadn't even begun.

Was it back to Square One...

She soon realized the mission had served its purpose. It wasn't the end —it was a stepping stone. A necessary chapter on the path to true financial freedom—divinely aligned to fulfill the purpose.

So, with this newfound freedom and the collapse of the bridge that got her here, she didn't fall or break down. She rose stronger—softer in spirit, sharper in vision. This time, she would build back better. Not from fear— but from *foundation and experience*. She was ready.

Now, her new path unfolded with clarity. This time, she set out to build **two income streams side by side while** reigniting her private investigations and security company. Within eight months, she had built two companies online to a top-tier position as a serial entrepreneur, as her business started to take off again.

Tirelessly building. Quietly succeeding. She began earning **thousands upon thousands weekly**—far surpassing anything her traditional businesses had ever paid her. This time, she was playing a different game.

Life was good. Lessons had been learned. Money was rolling in. She was debt-free, mortgage-free, and owned everything. No longer did her family ever have to suffer.

Then, one ordinary day, her husband looked at her with something more than love—**pride**. "You did it," he said. "I'm proud of you—always have been, always will be."

She smiled, soft and steady. Then he added, almost playfully, "Given your prayers are that powerful... maybe you should pray for a decentralized bank. We need one of those."

She burst out laughing. "What do you think I am?" she said. "Wonder

Woman? A magician? What am I supposed to do, whip out my magic wand?"

But even as the laughter lingered, something deeper stirred. It *resonated*. Not just as a laughing matter, but as a seed. And something in her spirit whispered back: *Why not? Another lifeline, perhaps?*

THE PRAYER THAT SHIFTED EVERYTHING

So, she prayed again. Not for fame or fortune, but for something far more powerful—a **decentralized, bankless system.** One that aligned with her values. One that could expand her vision and support the growing organization she was quietly rebuilding.

She prayed for a *new way* forward. Not to replace the system, but to create **a choice** within it. Even though she was now debt-free, she wanted more. She wanted **custodianship**—true autonomy over her own money, her path, her legacy.

Life was moving fast—and for the first time in a long time, it felt beautifully aligned. She had just launched a national tour across Australia, sharing her story and igniting hearts with her message of **financial freedom, decentralized empowerment,** and **blockchain innovation.** Her mission was bold, yet simple: to help everyday people reclaim *hope*—and reconnect to a freedom that couldn't be taken, controlled, or restricted.

As she boarded her flight for the next city, a familiar nervousness settled in. Flying had always unsettled her. But still, she showed up with whispered prayers slipping through trembling lips as she fastened her seatbelt. And then—**her phone lit up.** A message. From someone unexpected... but familiar.

An old friend. Trusted. Respected. Someone who had witnessed her journey from the sidelines. His words were genuine and proud. "**Congratulations. I've been watching what you're doing—it's powerful.**"

And then—he opened a door. A rare invitation. A chance to be part of something few even knew existed. A solution that echoed everything she had been praying for. A way to help people access new forms of financial independence *without rejecting what already exists*—but simply **giving them more choice.**

"What is it?" she asked, her mind hesitating, her heartbeat quickening.

His reply came in two words: **"Sixth Society." An exclusive, invite-only membership built on the blockchain.** An angel syndicate and tech lab providing a community of early adopters—those seeking access to real-world asset-backed startup projects, cutting-edge innovation, and the future of decentralized technology in the Web3 space.

Not hype. This was real infrastructure. Knowledge. Access. Custodianship. She sat with it for a moment, intrigued. **"Name one project that Sixth Society is doing,"** she replied.

The words appeared like a shooting star. **A fully decentralized, bankless software—designed to give people back their financial freedom.** A system with no middlemen. She froze for a moment—heart racing, spirit still. This was what she had prayed for, another lifeline, another need.

Within seconds, she saw the possibilities. With B2B functionality, she could register her **private investigation and security company** directly into the system—creating a business account that aligned with her values of custodianship and freedom. This wasn't just an opportunity—it was alignment. And she felt it in her bones: **Freedom was no longer just a hope. It was here.** Then he mentioned something else—quietly, almost like a dream.

There was a **founding membership.** Limited to only **500 people in the world.** A private community of visionaries, daring entrepreneurs, and investors—early believers granted exclusive access to opportunities most would never even hear about. She knew immediately that this was her doorway, her calling! There was no hesitation. **"Yes, absolutely! Yes!"** she said. **"How do I become one of the founding members?"**

And just as the plane began to ascend, the message thread went silent. She leaned back into her seat, staring out the window, her mind and heart in disbelief. The fear that usually gripped her on flights... wasn't there. Instead, she felt a sense of calm wrapped around her like a blanket of knowing.

This was no longer just something she had hoped for, prayed for, or even dared to imagine—this was her reality. And it was bigger than winning the lottery. The universe hadn't ignored her prayers. It had *redirected* them. A dream she had never dared to imagine was now **becoming her reality.**

Upon arriving at her destination, the moment her feet touched the ground, she grabbed her phone and called her husband, her voice trembling—not from fear, but from pure, overwhelming excitement.

"I've just been handed the very thing I've been praying for. Ready for it?"

Her husband waited in silence on the other end.

"A fully decentralized, bankless solution," she continued. "A new doorway. A chance to be part of something bigger than anything I've ever done in my life."

Her husband smiled on the other end.

This was the moment everything shifted. There wasn't a second to waste. She moved fast. No hesitation or second-guessing.

She messaged her contact with conviction: **"Let me in."**

This wasn't just a sign-up or an entry form. It was a *vetting process*—designed to ensure only the most aligned, committed visionaries were brought into the fold. This wasn't just another opportunity. This was destiny in motion.

And after everything she had walked through, fought for, and risen from—it became official. She had secured her place as **one of the 500 Founding Members of Sixth Society.** She stepped into it boldly, fully aware of what she was now part of. This wasn't just rare. It was revolutionary.

She became an official Founding Member of Sixth Society—in June of 2023. It was a title she wore not with ego, but with *fierce responsibility*. This wasn't just a new chapter. It was a new blueprint—a gateway to exclusive access and early-stage blockchain opportunities, grounded in real-world impact. It was more than access. **It was her calling.**

In the month that followed, **one of her online businesses collapsed**—and the second? **Reduced to rubble not long after.**

A brutal repeat of the past.

But this time, something was different. She had **Sixth Society.**

And deep down, she knew—those businesses weren't losses. They were **clearing the path.**

The breakdown before the breakthrough. And this time—**she was ready.**

She grasped the position and moved into Sixth Society like it was already her home. She stepped into it fully aware that she wasn't just meant to join the community. She was meant to help build it from the ground up.

And that's exactly what she did—*moving forward with purpose. With precision. With unwavering belief in what was possible.* She didn't just want to be in the room. **She wanted to embody the mission.** She decided she wasn't just going to dream about becoming a centimillionaire—**she was going to become one. She wanted to be one of the centimillionaires within her founding membership position. She took movement in.** Walking it. Breathing it. Living it.

Followed by taking the stage—not to speak, but to ignite. She led events—not to teach, but to awaken. She shared her story—not for applause, but for *impact.*

Then came **London, 2023**: her first global event. Nervous. Excited. Alive. Had she conquered her fear of flying? **Yes.** Because purpose is louder than fear, and she knew she was in true alignment when she released that fear.

One breakthrough led to the next. Then came **Miami, June 2024**: Another city. Another stage. A bigger mission. A bolder message. She was rising internally. Globally recognized amongst followers. Spiritually anchored. Ready for more.

But just as she was stepping into her next level—**Life hit pause.**

Tragedy struck. A car accident. A moment that could have ended everything. Pain struck her whole body, with numbness running down her face, arms, and legs. She lay still as the doctor strapped her body down so that she could not move and secured a brace around her neck.

She asked for a mirror to see. The label read: MIAMI BRACE. And in that moment, her world shifted again. She lay there, unmoving, staring at the ceiling, thinking of the name of the brace that had Miami stitched around her neck. The irony wasn't lost on her. She had arrived with clarity, with fire in her soul, and a deep belief in who she was. She was ready —ready to expand her mission, to walk boldly in the fullness of her purpose.

And then, in a single moment, **life slammed on the brakes.**

The body that once moved with power and intention... was now still. The mind that once thought ten steps ahead... was now forced to surrender to the moment. And yet—*something sacred stirred within her.*

This wasn't the end. It was a pause. A holy interruption. She knew there was a lesson in everything she had been through, and this was no exception.

This wouldn't break her. It would **build her again. Deeper. Wiser. Even stronger.**

There, in the stillness, she met herself again. Not the public version of the founding member or the private investigator. Not the speaker. Not the builder or strategist.

Just the woman. Bruised, quiet, cracked open. Held by something bigger than logic. She didn't rush to "get back." She listened. To her breath. To her body. To the voice within. Her husband was by her side, keeping her grounded and centered. He was her anchor.

This wasn't just about healing physically or mentally—**it was a recalibration. A divine reset. A warrior's silence before the next roar.** And when she rose, she would rise differently. Not to prove. Not to perform. But to *embody* the next evolution of who she was always born to be.

Her message now—clearer than ever:

Freedom is more than a financial goal. It's a spiritual state. And it begins within.

They said she might not make it to the Sixth Society global event in Miami. She knew the doctors were wrong. She would focus on the positive, not the pain. Ignore what the doctors are saying—they don't know who you are. So when the doctors repeatedly said, "No, you will not be traveling," she said, **"Yes—watch me."**

Every scar told a story. Every fall taught her how to rise. Every thought was a battlefield. And through every storm, she was reminded: **Warriors don't wait. They walk through the fire, more determined, more charged.**

This is your reminder that power doesn't come from having all the answers or having it all.

It comes from refusing to give up when the world hands you every reason to.

It comes from choosing to seek opportunities when others retreat.

From surrounding yourself with visionaries who see beyond the noise.

From standing with those who are building what's next—with integrity, with intention, and with impact.

This is not your end. It's your ignition point. It's the moment your story pivots. And it starts right now—with you choosing to rise. Because once you hit rock bottom, the only way is up.

YOUR MIND IS A BATTLEFIELD

There came a moment where everything in her life could have shattered her—financial collapse, shame, fear, and the kind of heavy silence that screams in your soul. She stood at a crossroads: surrender to the pain, or rise and fight. She could've chosen to let the world win. But she didn't because she learned something that changed everything:

The mind is the first battlefield.
And if you don't take control of it, you lose before you ever begin.
You either get up and eat—or you get eaten.
She chose to fight. To hunt. To rise. To eat.

SURROUND YOURSELF WITH DOERS

When the sky was falling, there was one voice that remained steady: her husband. He was more than just a soulmate—he was her pillar, her strongest supporter, the love that fueled her fire. He reminded her of her greatness when she forgot, even when times got tough. His belief in her created the wind that fueled her fire.

She chose to surround herself with people who were building, not breaking. Dreaming, not doubting. Doers, not talkers. Givers, not takers. Because in this game, energy is everything. And when you're surrounded by warriors, you rise like one too. She knew that you attract what you are. And she became a magnet to greatness, surrounded by those who shared her vision and were ready to rise together.

She led teams while battling storms no one else could see. She closed deals while her body screamed for rest. She ran events while her family cried out for her presence. She held meetings with a broken soul—smiling on the outside while breaking on the inside behind closed doors. She would wipe tears minutes before doing Zoom calls, yet still represent. All the while, the world applauded her strength, never knowing the war she was quietly fighting. Why is that? Because real warriors show up—not when it is easy, but when it matters.

FROM CRISIS TO CUSTODIAN: THE RISE OF A WARRIOR WOMAN

HER WORDS

She didn't just rebuild; she *reinvented*. And she's bringing as many people with her as she can. Her mission is to awaken others to their power. To help them realize that this isn't just about survival anymore. It's about kicking that next door wide open and saying, "I'm here. And I'm building a future no one saw coming." And for every person that didn't believe in her, she is thankful, as they drove her to move forward with vision and purpose and an unbreakable spirit.

A NEW DOOR: SIXTH SOCIETY

That hunger led her to something bigger. It led her to a doorway she hadn't expected—into a space where innovation met purpose, and community met calling. With Sixth Society, she became part of something that could never be replicated. An invitation for those who could see what others couldn't. A chance to access what most could only dream of.

She had received a once-in-a-lifetime **invitation**: not just to witness the future of decentralized finance, but to help build it from the ground up as a founding member. She recognized the magnitude of it instantly. This wasn't just another business. It was a calling. A world that once felt unreachable became a space she proudly called home.

For her, it was attunement. A place where her ambition was not only accepted but *nurtured*...

Where her vision was not only supported but also *propelled forward*. It felt like she had stepped into another realm. A world within a world. Built around solving real problems—not speculating on trends.

Members didn't just gain access. They gained community and alignment. To knowledge. To meaningful connections. To early-stage innovations quietly shaping the world to come. There were no gimmicks. No empty promises. Only visionaries—bold enough to see what's next and brave enough to help build it. And in that space, she knew—she was exactly where she was meant to be.

TRUSTYFY: PURPOSE MEETS PRACTICALITY

Alongside Sixth Society, she champions Trustyfy—a blockchain-based software platform designed to bridge the gap between centralized and decentralized systems. Trustyfy helps people organize their digital wallets, manage multi-user access, and reclaim financial autonomy in a world that often feels overwhelming.

It's intuitive. Secure. Designed with simplicity in mind—even Grandma could use it.

This journey was never just about access or money. It was about *freedom*—with innovation, with sovereignty, and with the future she envisioned. For the past two years, she's worked quietly on the frontlines—hosting gatherings, running private events, and showing up where it mattered most.

Now, that mission is expanding. She's honored to represent both Sixth Society and Trustyfy at international blockchain events—sharing space with aligned voices who believe in innovation with *intention*, decentralization with *integrity*, and technology with *impact*. From intimate roundtables to global stages, she contributes to conversations shaping what's next. With clarity. With courage. And with the quiet confidence of someone who's walked through fire.

LEGACY IN MOTION

Just when she thought her story was complete, another chapter was already being written.

While she remained fully immersed in the evolution of Sixth Society and Trustyfy—two powerful pillars that she was proud to be a founding member of—she also birthed something far more personal: **EighthRealm**.

EighthRealm wasn't just a clothing brand. It was a living legacy—a movement she was building thread by thread with her family. Each product tells a story. Each design carries intention. It became a reflection of everything she once longed for: strength, belief, and soul-deep purpose. It was her answer to the hunger for truth and inner meaning. A way to build a future worth inheriting—with her husband and children at the center of it all.

Her children are learning how to create and build from the trenches up—to earn their stripes through effort, not entitlement. Legacy isn't what you leave behind—it's what you build together. You can build and lead with your soul and still create success that lasts generations. She didn't just write her story—she transformed it into a foundation her children would grow from and something others could wear, believe in, and rise with.

Prayer remained her rhythm, not as survival, but as sacred fuel. Every word she spoke became a compass. Every step, a message. This wasn't just about business. It was about holding higher standards. Living at a higher frequency. Becoming the very words you speak.

She realized, looking back, that each realm mirrored a part of her rise. From pain to purpose. From survival to sovereignty. And so, the Eight Realms of EighthRealm were born—not as an idea, but as the very essence of her journey and her family's continuous journey together. This was a soul-led path of leadership, legacy, and inner power. Each realm represents a stage of becoming. A journey inward and upward. A process of growth—until you arrive at the eighth level: the realm of full ownership, divine alignment, and unstoppable soul leadership.

Realm 1: Survival
The realm of beginnings.
Where pain births purpose.
This is where she learns how to endure the fire—when life gives her no choice but to fight. This is the realm of the trenches, where strength is forged in silence, and grit becomes her greatest weapon.

Realm 2: Awakening
The moment she realizes she was born for more.
She stops numbing, stops hiding, and begins to feel again.
In this realm, her soul whispers louder than her fear. She begins to question the system, the stories, and the silence—and starts to see the truth.

Realm 3: Discipline
The realm of work, structure, and daily decisions.
She learns that becoming isn't about motivation—it's about consistency.
This is where she builds, raises standards, and becomes accountable to her vision, not her excuses.

Realm 4: Courage
This is where she starts speaking up and showing up.
She starts building, even if no one claps.
In this realm, she breaks free from people-pleasing and claims her voice, her path, her birthright.

Realm 5: Vision
The realm of clarity.
She sees the life she's building and why. She no longer chases trends—she creates movements.
This is where she becomes the architect of her legacy, designing from the soul, not from survival.

Realm 6: Leadership
The realm of responsibility.
She stops blaming. She starts leading.
She becomes the person others look to—not for attention, but for alignment.
Here, she embodies her values and carries the weight of the mission with humility and fire.

Realm 7: Impact
This is where her work becomes bigger than just her.
She starts transforming lives, building systems, and creating ripple effects.
She mentors. She multiplies. She moves mountains—not for praise, but for purpose.

Realm 8: Sovereignty
The final realm. The awakening of full embodiment.
She is no longer chasing—she is.
She leads with soul, builds with her power, and owns her identity with no apology.
She is financially sovereign, spiritually aligned, emotionally whole.
This is legacy.
This is generational transformation.
This is EighthRealm.

EighthRealm is a way of life. It's the soul's return to truth—threaded through every product, every message, every move. This is for the ones who build from nothing—and turn it into everything. EighthRealm became the wearable embodiment of that journey—every piece, a thread of truth, stitched with legacy and soul.

Each of her children holds a realm within. One mirrors her grit. One reflects her awakening. One carries her vision further than she ever dreamed. And together, they hold the rhythm of her legacy.

With her husband always beside her—aligned in love, connected in soul, and united in vision—they are building EighthRealm not just as a brand but as a sanctuary for their children to grow, lead, and rise.

This isn't just her blueprint. It's yours. For every man and woman rising. For every child watching. For every family growing. For everyone rebuilding from nothing. The EighthRealm is for them, too.

ENTER: THE RISE OF LITTLE JIT—THE LITTLE WARRIORS WITHIN

From all she had walked through, something sacred emerged—something for the children. Little Jit wasn't just a brand her children would wear underneath the banner of eighthrealm. It was a soulful imprint, a reflection of everything she wanted to pass down. Little Jit carries the codes, the grit, and the essence of legacy in motion. It represents learning through example, rising with soul, and teaching the next generation how to lead from the inside out. It's not just something to wear—it's something to feel.

Little Jit was inspired by *all* her children. By their hearts, their voices, their untamed spirit. Their soul-led power shaped every thread, every design, every intention. It has become a movement for future rising leaders—streetwear for kids who walk with purpose. Something bold. Something real.

She was raising her children to be divinely crafted originals who didn't need handouts or applause. Just raw ability, grounded truth, and the kind of self-worth you can't buy or fake. They weren't built to fit in. They were built to stand out. Born to build. Born to rise.

CONCLUSION: YOUR JOURNEY BEGINS NOW

This isn't the end of the story—it's just the beginning. You've already made it this far. You're a warrior, a dreamer, a leader. The question is, What are you going to do next? The path ahead won't always be easy—but it's yours. Step into your power and begin building the life and legacy you were born for. When you're ready to turn inspiration into action, know this: You won't be walking alone.

She had already seen the vision—clear as day. She knows she will be one of the next unknown centimillionaires. She knew wealth would come, but more importantly, she knew who she needed to become—and who her children needed to become—to hold it with purpose. Walking in divine alignment to teach her children the true meaning of what it takes to be successful and create wealth, no matter what the circumstances. To raise warriors. To raise soulful builders. To raise children who would know how to fight for a dream—not just receive one or give up when things got tough.

She never wanted to hand down riches without her children understanding the true meaning and value of money and what it took to create it. That's why she didn't protect them from the process—she invited them into it. She let them see the grind. The mess. The magic. The early mornings. The late nights. The breakdowns and breakthroughs putting it all together.

This is Sixth Society.
An angel syndicate. That provides exclusive membership access to knowledge, networking, seminars, and events, where start-ups pitch their business directly to the members.

This is Trustyfy.
A solution we have all been waiting for—to become the full custodian of your money, where nobody can freeze your account or block your transactions. A decentralized software solution bridging the gap between crypto and fiat with on and off ramping and a visa debit card to go spending with.

This is Eighth Realm.
A soul-led legacy—worn, lived, and passed down. Not stitched in trends, but in truth.
Built for the ones who remember who they are. A brand for those who carry fire in their hearts and purpose in their steps. A realm built from nothing to something.

Three Lanes. One Mission.
To build with purpose.
To lead with truth.
To rise with soul.
This is not the end.
This is the beginning of a new era—
One led by those bold enough to remember who they are.
One built by warriors, creators, and soul-led visionaries.
One designed to shift the system from the inside out.
This is her realm now. And she's building it—for all who dare to rise. Are you ready to rise, lead, and build your realm?

Nadia Jacobs is the kind of woman you'd go to war with—the kind empires rise with. Visionary in business, relentless in motherhood, and sovereign in soul. A strategist by design, a nurturer by nature, and a warrior by experience. She didn't just survive the system—she outgrew it, rebuilt it, and now leads others to do the same.

As the principal director of a leading investigation and K9 security company, with over a decade of experience in private investigations and high-level security—built alongside her husband—she has delivered critical risk management and investigative solutions consulting to clients from all walks of life worldwide. She thrives on all types of investigative and security requirements and has advanced-level training skills when it comes to K9 dog handling for high-risk jobs. Known as one of the leading women in her field, she brings not just experience but a solid presence and is trusted by individuals and institutions globally.

As a founding member of Sixth Society, an exclusive angel syndicate, Nadia stands at the forefront of blockchain, Web3, and decentralized innovations. She is actively helping roll out real-world technologies and strategic ventures. With years immersed in the blockchain and Web3 space, she is helping pioneer real-world, tech-incubated solutions. Just like their most recent incubated project called Trustyfy, she is helping by equipping people to become true custodians of their own money from B2C and B2B—bridging the gap between traditional finance and the decentralized future. Through Sixth Society, she opens the door for people to have access to early-stage blockchain ventures—an angel investor that gets exclusive access—that are typically only reserved for insiders.

For those wanting to understand more or get involved, Nadia Jacobs has created **Unbank Freedom,** which is a gateway platform designed to provide access to Sixth Society and their decentralized bankless solution, Trustyfy. Visitors can create a 100 percent decentralized, bankless account with just a click of a button at www.unbankfreedom.com—bridging the gap between centralized and decentralized systems in a way that complements both worlds, creating an account within seconds. Non-custodial by design—users retain full control over wallets, data, and access. Built for everyone—from individuals to businesses ready to scale. On-chain tools with real-world utility, including multi-signature wallets, permission-based access, real-time activity reports, and scalable features for corporate and business use.

Through Unbank Freedom, individuals and businesses can also book a direct consultation with Nadia to explore tailored pathways in this evolving space—including how to get involved with their invite-only private angel syndicate—Sixth Society. This offers aligned individuals the opportunity to request access to early-stage blockchain ventures, start-ups that have typically only ever been reserved for the privileged few.

Unbank Freedom isn't just a platform Nadia built—it's a door. One that opens into a new realm of leadership, strategic positioning, aligned ventures, next-level access, and real-world connectivity on the blockchain, like a real venture capitalist.

EighthRealm & Little Jit are due to launch officially in March 2026. Not just a clothing brand. A movement. A lifestyle. Designed to clothe the next generation in truth, courage, and legacy. Through EighthRealm, Nadia and her family will offer custom apparel that speaks of transformation, purpose, and power.

Whether you're:

- Seeking decentralized, bankless solutions
- Exploring high-level angel syndicate ventures with exclusive invite-only access
- Or wearing your story with pride through her custom apparel

Nadia is building the blueprint. Explore her vision and connect with her here:

Website: www.unbankfreedom.com

—

Instagram: @nadiaj_official

—

LinkedIn: www.linkedin.com/in/nadiajofficial

—

Telegram: @Nadiajofficial

Eighth Realm: eighthrealmofficial.com *(coming soon)*

Sign up for your FREE bankless account:
https://app.trustyfy.com?by=101aah

FORGED IN FIRE: RISING FROM THE ASHES OF CHAOS

BY SUZANNE M. SAUNDERS-O'HERRON, M.ED

There are moments in life when the heat feels unbearable—when everything you've built, everything you've clung to, begins to burn. We all know these moments. Moments of loss. Of betrayal. Of chaos so deep it makes you question whether you'll ever feel safe again. The kind of pain that doesn't just knock the wind out of you—it changes the rhythm of your heartbeat forever.

For some, those fires come later in life. For others, they begin the moment they arrive in this world. I was one of the latter.

My entry into life wasn't soft or sacred; it was a near miss. A mistake in the delivery room—a moment of mistaken identity between twin sisters—could have cost me my life before I had even drawn my first breath. On that day, though, fate intervened.

Long before that moment, the odds were already against me, and chaos was coming for me. My mother had taken a positive pregnancy test, only to be told shortly afterward that she wasn't pregnant. With a history of fertility challenges, she underwent two invasive procedures. The doctors found no egg and concluded it had been a chemical pregnancy or an early miscarriage.

But I was still there, growing quietly, unseen.

A short while later, my mother and her twin sister discovered they were both, in fact, pregnant, sending shockwaves through my grandparents and surprising my mother, who was determined to have been pregnant during her previously invasive procedures. As their pregnancies neared term, something incredible happened: They both went into labor on the same day.

My mother went into labor overnight—right on schedule. Hours later, my aunt, two weeks early and flagged as a high-risk pregnancy, began laboring as well. In the chaos, the hospital staff confused the twins and began treating my mother as the high-risk case, adding sensors and implementing more observational protocol than she would have otherwise received.

That unexpected error became my saving grace.

During the observational procedures, my heart rate began to plummet—dropping, then stopping altogether. Immediately, my mother was rushed in for an emergency C-section. That's when they discovered the umbilical cord wrapped tightly around my neck—multiple times. I was rushed to receive immediate treatment and diagnostic testing to ensure I was healthy, something there had not been a question about hours earlier had the mistaken identity leading to further observation not happened. It was later determined, had they allowed her to labor naturally, as was the original intent, the doctor said I likely wouldn't have survived.

In the midst of confusion and crisis, something greater stepped in. The mistaken identity ended up saving my life.

However, with that first breath I took earthside, I was thrown into the fire. From that day forward, it seemed like the flames never stopped. I've spent my entire life fighting. Fighting to be seen. Fighting to be heard. Fighting to pave my own way because I felt the "traditional route" was never going to be in my favor. Fighting to exist in a world that, for reasons I may never fully understand, seemed hellbent on breaking me.

I grew up in a home dimmed by addiction and fractured by dysfunction. Hunger wasn't just about empty cupboards. It was a longing for safety; for peace; for something that felt like love. If not for my grandparents stepping in and lifting me out of that darkness, I honestly don't know where I'd be today. I was just a child, yet already carrying a weight that could crush a grown adult. I became a fighter before I learned to read and write. I learned to smile through bruises, to act strong through screams, and to hold everything in while holding everyone else up. I created a safe space in my mind —one where I could escape any time I was experiencing too much pain or strife—a world free from the horrors I was enduring. I carried that safe space into adulthood and recognized its existence during the times I was going through traumatic experiences. Sadly, I realized as an adult, trauma didn't wait until I was grown. Instead, it shaped me while I was still growing and learning the rules of the world. I recognize now, the trauma I endured should have swallowed me whole. I was bullied relentlessly, especially by family members and abused in ways that no child, no human, should ever have to endure. Mentally. Emotionally. Physically. Sexually. While all that was happening, I was expected to care for others, to be strong, and to survive. The lingering question for me became, "How do you survive when you're still trying to understand what it means to live?"

When you realize no one else is coming to save you, you have to learn to save yourself.

Today, I look into the eyes of my children, particularly, the two children I've taken into my home; children who now call me *Mom*. I see reflections of my own journey in their silent wounds and in the heavy histories they carry. Their biological father—lost to addiction and violence. Their mother—behind bars for her role in his death. They battle the constant ebb and flow of nature versus nurture, and obtain diagnosis after diagnosis that would cause most to want to give up. Yet here they are. Still standing. Still trying. Still fighting.

Just like I did.

The battles never stopped for me. I've stood in a courtroom, testifying during a manslaughter trial. I've faced my own cancer scares, staring at the unknown with trembling hands. I've watched my husband flatline beside me while I was driving on the highway, as I pounded his chest and tried to keep us both alive. I have had roofs literally cave in on me—three separate times—like life wanted to make sure I didn't forget just how fragile safety can be. I have faced death more times than I can count, including while bringing my miracle baby into the world. A miracle baby who, too, fights every day to survive and battle the cards that have been stacked against him. From death threats to breaking both legs, both wrists and ending up in a wheelchair, I recognize there are so many things that should have shattered me. Yet somehow, they didn't.

In the darkest moments of my life (the kind that steals your breath and blurs the edges of everything you thought you knew), I've found myself staring into the void, asking one haunting question: *Who am I, really?*

Not in the surface-level sense of roles or titles (daughter, partner, professional) but in the stripped-down, soul-baring way that confronts you when the lights go out and the silence is loud. I've sat alone with my thoughts, unraveling the memories and wounds, wondering if I am nothing more than the sum of what has happened to me—the sum of the trauma, abandonment, betrayals, and heartbreaks I never saw coming. I've asked myself if I've been permanently shaped by pain—if the girl who once dreamed big and believed in magic got buried under the weight of it all. I've questioned whether the damage defines me. Whether I'm destined to repeat the same patterns. Whether hope, for someone like me, is foolish—or if there's still a way to rise, rebuild, and reclaim the parts of me I thought were lost.

Somewhere in the ache, in the deafening silence, a whisper remains. A fragile and flickering, but defiant, belief that I am not just what's been done to me. That there is something unbreakable at my core. That even in my most shattered state, there is still room to become. To evolve. To write a new chapter that doesn't erase what I've endured but rises from it with deeper strength, softer wisdom, and wilder grace.

It took years for me to realize the duality of my existence. I am not only what happened to me, but I am also what I choose to do with it.

In that reflection, I've learned that the most meaningful qualifications in life don't come from degrees or résumés. They come from sleepless nights. From moments I was broken but still showed up. From the fire that kept coming—and the strength that kept rising.

The story I carry is not a list of tragedies. It's a roadmap of resilience, a blueprint of becoming. In the deepest parts of that story, I've found my voice—not a loud one, not always polished—but true. In telling it, I've learned that I'm not alone.

There is power in speaking about what once brought shame. There is healing in letting go of guilt. There is strength in honoring emotions that were once buried to make others comfortable. I no longer hide behind "I'm fine." I no longer chase perfection. I show up real—tears, truth, trembling voice, and all.

Boundaries became my bridge to peace. Saying no became a sacred act of self-respect. Releasing relationships that drained me wasn't selfish—it was necessary. Choosing alignment over approval has now saved me more times than I can count, even when I am not always perfect at it.

Faith, too, carried me. Not the loud kind or the kind tied to ritual or dogma. Instead, it was the quiet knowing that I was never walking alone. That the doors that opened weren't a coincidence. That grace found me as I cried in my car in gas station parking lots, in the kindness of strangers' words, and in the silence of my own breath. That something bigger—call it God, call it the universe, call it purpose—was always guiding me forward.

Now, I try to use every scar, every setback, and every chapter I once wanted to erase, to guide and support others. I mentor. I lead. I speak up. I advocate. I become, every single day, what I once needed.

The lessons came hard—but they came. I've stopped waiting for purpose to show up. I try to create it now—every day. From the way I speak to my children to how I show up for others and in the way I say yes to healing and no to chaos.

Every day I am working on redefining success for myself and breaking generational curses. It's not the loud wins that mean the most to me, I have started to realize. No, instead it's the quiet ones—the days I show up even when I don't feel like it. With deep breaths and tearful prayers, it's the one small step forward after two steps back, and the deep-seeded recognition that it all counts. Every single bit.

I am still here. So are you. That means something.

You are not behind. You are not broken. You are *becoming*.

Let your pain be your teacher. Let your fire be your forge. Let your truth be your guide.

When you feel like stopping, remember this:

You didn't come this far to hide now. You are not just surviving. You are rising.

Sometimes, when I pause to look back on everything I've survived, even I find it hard to believe. It feels like the script of someone else's life. But no, it's just me. Still here. Still standing.

Not because I'm unbreakable. I've broken more times than I can admit.

Not because I never fall apart. I fall often. I cry. I scream. I question everything. One thing remains true beyond all of that, though: I refuse to stay down.

Even as I juggle multiple jobs, run businesses, volunteer, pursue a doctorate, raise children, try to be a supportive and loving wife, and somehow hold space for others in crisis—I carry a truth that keeps me going: **I was made for more than survival.**

People often ask how I do it. I laugh, usually shrug, and say, "I have no idea. And I'm not doing it well."

The truth is this: I do it because I must.

I do it because something inside me refuses to quit. Maybe it's faith. Maybe it's the sheer, stubborn refusal to let the fire win. Maybe it's the deep knowing that this life—my life—is not over yet.

My grandfather used to say, "An object in motion stays in motion."

So, I keep moving.

Resilience, I've learned, isn't just about surviving the fire—it's about learning how to rise from it.

This isn't just a roadmap. It's a reminder—for you and for me—that the fire does not have the final say.

We do.

RISE FROM THE FIRE AND KEEP GOING

Choose Purpose Over Pain

Pain is inevitable. It reaches everyone at some point, creeping into the corners of our lives when we least expect it. Allowing pain to define you, though—to become the core of who you are—is a choice.

I've seen what happens when people let their suffering consume them. They become trapped in a cycle of hopelessness, believing their hardships and victimhood are the only story they will ever tell. They start to identify more with their wounds than with their ability to heal. Their past becomes a prison, and every painful experience only tightens the chains.

That's not my story.

Instead of letting pain diminish me, I have chosen, as difficult as it is, to transform it into something powerful. I take what was meant to break me and use it as the foundation for something greater. I let my struggles shape me, but not define me.

I channel my trauma into advocacy for mental health, using my voice to uplift others who are still in the trenches. I mentor those who feel lost, just as I once did, and surround myself with my own mentors who lift me when I fall back into those familiar depths of despair and uncertainty. I work with others to create opportunities for healing, empowerment, and hope.

The very experiences that were supposed to destroy me have now become my greatest sources of strength.

I had to learn how to turn my pain into purpose, and that transformation doesn't happen overnight. It requires intentional effort and a deep willingness to shift your mindset. No matter where you are in your journey, you have the power to reclaim your story.

One of the most powerful things you can do is take control of your narrative. In other words, own your story by turning your wounds into wisdom.

Your pain, your struggles, and your experiences don't make you weak—they make you *human*. When you share your story, you not only empower yourself but also give others permission to do the same.

OWN YOUR STORY

Turn Wounds into Wisdom

There are parts of your story that you've probably hidden—not because they don't matter, but because they matter so much. The ones that still sting when you think about them. The ones you've carried quietly, afraid of what others might say if they ever came to light. Maybe someone made you believe those parts of you were too messy, too painful, too much. The truth is, **the very parts you're afraid to share are the ones someone else is silently waiting to hear.** We all have chapters that never make it into casual conversation—the heartbreaks, the losses, the failures, the moments of shame or regret, or the miracles that happened behind closed doors. While they may not always be easy to talk about, they are the stories that shaped us into who we are.

When we choose to speak those truths out loud—with vulnerability, courage, and honesty—we stop pretending. We stop performing. In doing so, we free ourselves from the weight of silence—and we give others permission to do the same. Someone out there is walking a path you have already survived. Someone is looking for a sign that healing is real, that brokenness doesn't have to be the end, and that it's possible to rise from the parts of your story you thought would destroy you. Owning your truth doesn't mean reliving your pain—it means standing in it, fully, and saying, "This is part of me, and I'm still standing."

I've learned that one of the most radical acts of self-love is telling the truth—**especially the kind that isn't polished or pretty.** There's power in saying, "This happened. I felt it. I lived through it. I'm still here." When you show up with honesty, you become a lighthouse—not just for yourself, but for others who are still lost in their storm. There is strength in being real. There is healing in being seen. There is unmatched freedom in finally letting go of the need to pretend.

There is power in what you've been through. Power in every scar, every setback, and every dark chapter that you somehow lived through. Yet, so many of us keep those parts locked away, as if silence can somehow make the past disappear.

But silence doesn't heal. Honesty does. When you begin to own your story—not just the polished parts, but the raw, the messy, the broken pieces—you begin to reclaim your life. You stop letting your past define you, and you start letting it refine you. Your story matters. Not in spite of the pain, but because of it. When you turn your wounds into wisdom, you don't just heal yourself—you create space for others to do the same.

Let this be the moment you stop hiding.

Let this be the moment you own it all.

Not because it's easy, but because it's freeing.

Think back to a time when you felt alone in your pain. What would have made a difference for you? Who did you need in that moment? Now, become that person for someone else.

In Your Personal Life: Stop hiding your past as if it's something to be ashamed of. Every struggle, every setback, every moment of doubt has shaped the person you are today. Owning your story means accepting it—not just the victories, but the scars, too. Speak your truth. Whether it's through journaling, therapy, or simply having honest conversations with trusted people, acknowledging your journey is the first step toward healing.

In Your Professional Life: People connect with authenticity. Whether you're leading a team, running a business, or working in a corporate setting, vulnerability builds trust. Sharing your journey—how you overcame obstacles, how you built resilience—makes you a more effective leader, mentor, or business owner. Use your experiences to cultivate connections rooted in authenticity. In leadership, storytelling is one of the most powerful tools to inspire and engage others. Don't be afraid to share moments of struggle that have shaped your resilience—it makes you more relatable and real.

Ask yourself: What part of my story am I afraid to share? How could that part help someone else feel less alone? We all have stories we try to hide—the moments we wish we could rewrite, the pain we've buried deep because facing it feels too heavy. The truth is, those very wounds we avoid? They hold the seeds of our greatest strength. What parts of my story have shaped my strength? How can sharing them help others?

EMBRACE THE POWER OF STORYTELLING

Your Voice is Your Strength

There's a reason stories move us—they remind us we are not alone. Somewhere, someone is carrying a weight that feels unbearable, believing they're the only one who's ever felt that broken. But when you share your story—your real, raw, unfiltered truth—you offer them a lifeline. You become proof that survival is possible. That healing is possible. That forward is possible. For years, I believed my pain was mine alone to carry. I feared that speaking it out loud would make me look weak or invite judgment I wasn't ready to face. So I stayed silent, locked in my own narrative. But eventually, the silence became heavier than the story itself.

When I finally began to speak—first in whispers, then in sentences, then in bold declarations of truth—I realized something powerful: My story wasn't just mine. It was a mirror for others. A light for someone still walking through the dark. A permission slip for others to release their shame and speak their own truth. Each time I opened up, I freed another part of myself—and in the process, gave others the courage to do the same.

Because our voices are not burdens—they are bridges. Our stories are not liabilities—they are tools for connection, for compassion, for change.

You don't need a stage or an audience to make a difference. You just need the courage to be real. The more you embrace your story, the more you step into your power. When you use your voice with intention, you don't just rewrite your own narrative—you help someone else believe they can, too. That's the power of storytelling. That's the strength of your voice.

YOUR STORY SHAPES YOUR FUTURE

Your story holds power, but only if you're willing to speak it. The experiences you've lived through, the battles you've fought, and the wisdom you've gained weren't meant to stay locked away. They were meant to serve. To inspire. To connect. Because someone out there needs to hear what you've survived. Your truth might be the very thing that unlocks healing for someone else.

Your voice is one of the most powerful forces you carry. So choose to speak your truth with courage and with discernment. Let it reflect where you're headed, not where you've been. When you honor your story, you create a life that heals, grows, and transforms—one aligned step at a time.

ADVOCATE FOR WHAT YOU ONCE NEEDED

Think back to your hardest moments—the ones that nearly broke you. The nights you cried quietly so no one would hear. The days you smiled through pain, hoping someone, anyone, would notice that you were barely holding on. Maybe no one came. Maybe you had to walk that road alone, without a guide, without a voice to comfort you, without the reassurance that you were worthy of love, safety, or support. Maybe—just maybe—that's exactly why you're here now. Not just to survive what you've been through, but to **become what you once needed.** To be the person you were waiting for. To speak the words you longed to hear. To offer the support you never received.

There's a sacred kind of purpose that's born from unmet needs. When you choose to transform your pain into passion, your isolation into empathy, your silence into advocacy, you don't just heal your own heart. You become the bridge for someone else's. You create space for others to feel seen, heard, and held. You remind them they're not alone. And in doing so, you don't just rewrite your own story—you help others write a new one, too.

You are living proof that healing is possible. That rising is possible. So don't let what hurt you become the end of your story. **Let it become the beginning of someone else's hope—and the catalyst for the change you were always meant to make.**

In Your Personal Life: Support a cause that resonates with your experiences. Volunteer, donate, or simply lend an ear to someone who is walking the path you once traveled. Whether it's advocating for mental health, supporting survivors, or mentoring young people, your lived experiences make you uniquely qualified to help others.

In Your Professional Life: Create spaces for support and advocacy in your workplace. If you struggle with burnout, advocate for better work-life balance. If you face discrimination, push for diversity and inclusion initiatives. If you lacked mentorship, be the leader you once needed. One of the greatest teachers and leaders I ever worked for is someone who embodies this very principle. She had horrible experiences with her previous leaders, and as such, vowed to be different for her employees. Do as she did. Turn that pain and suffering you may have endured at the hands of a former leader or manager and instead transform yourself into something far different than they were.

Ask yourself: What gap in support did I once experience? How can I fill that gap for someone else?

Your struggles have given you skills that no classroom ever could. Resilience, adaptability, emotional intelligence—these are invaluable strengths that set you apart.

YOUR STRUGGLES ARE NOT PROOF OF ABANDONMENT

They Are Proof of Strength

It's easy to look at your life, especially during the hardest moments, and ask, *Why me?* Why does it seem like others have smoother paths while yours is filled with detours, obstacles, and unexpected storms? But what if the struggles you've endured aren't signs that you've been abandoned—

they're signs that you've been **prepared.** Every battle you've fought, every heartbreak you've survived, every painful season you've walked through has shaped you into someone stronger, wiser, and more grounded than you were before. These experiences didn't come to destroy you—they came to deepen you.

You are not weak because of what you've been through. **You are strong because of it.** You've faced storms that could have easily crushed someone else, and yet, here you are—still standing. That kind of resilience doesn't come from ease; it comes from perseverance. And that is not an accident. That is not proof of failure or divine neglect. That is **proof of purpose.** You've been refined, not rejected. Shaped, not shattered. Everything you've overcome has prepared you for what's next. And that strength? It's your reminder that you were never meant to break—you were meant to rise.

SHIFT YOUR MINDSET FROM "WHY ME?" TO "WHAT NOW?"

When life hurts—really hurts—it's natural to ask why. Why me? Why this? Why now? Why did I have to be the one who lost so much, who carried this kind of pain, whose story started in brokenness? These are fair questions. They're deeply human. We all wrestle with them when our hearts are cracked open by loss, trauma, betrayal, or disappointment. But eventually—after the dust settles, after the grief shifts from sharp to heavy—you're faced with a different question. Not "Why me?" but "What now?" What do I do with everything I've been through? What can I take from this? Who might I become because of it?

This isn't about pretending everything happens for a reason. Some things just hurt. Some chapters are cruel, unfair, and senseless. If you're still here, there's still purpose inside of you. I've asked "Why me?" more times than I can count. For a long time, I stayed stuck there—believing that if I could just figure out the reason, maybe the pain would make more sense.

I never found the answer I was looking for. What I found instead was a choice: to let my pain define me or to let it refine me. To stay bitter or to grow deeper. To keep reliving the question or to start creating the answer.

"Why me?" keeps us tethered to the past. But "What now?" pulls us toward the future. And no matter what you've been through, your future still matters. Even if your healing is messy. Even if you're still unsure of what it will look like. So ask yourself—not with pressure, but with permission: *What now? What next? What could rise from this that never could have grown in comfort?* You may not get the answer right away. But asking the question? That's where the healing begins.

In Your Personal Life: Every hardship you have endured has given you wisdom. Maybe it's made you a better parent, a more understanding friend, or someone who can now guide others through similar struggles. Your pain was not for nothing—find a way to turn it into purpose.

In Your Professional Life: If you've faced failures, challenges, or setbacks in your career, use them as lessons rather than defeats. The most successful people aren't those who never fail—they're the ones who learn from every failure and keep going.

Ask yourself: How can I use my experiences to help someone else? How can I turn my challenges into stepping stones instead of roadblocks?

YOU ARE STILL HERE

And That Means Something

If life were trying to break you, it would have done so by now. But it didn't. You're still standing—maybe not unscarred, maybe not unchanged, but *still here*. And that alone means something. It means your journey isn't over. It means there is still work for you to do, someone you are meant to impact, and a purpose that's calling your name even if you haven't fully heard it yet. The pain you've endured is not the period at the end of your sentence—it's the beginning of a strength that's still unfolding. So, keep going. Keep believing. Keep trusting that even in the chaos, even in the moments that make no sense at all, something greater is at work on your behalf. Because **you are still here—and that means your purpose is, too.**

KEEP MOVING FORWARD, NO MATTER HOW HARD IT GETS

Life is unpredictable. Some days, moving forward looks like launching a new business, making a bold career move, or taking a major step toward your dreams. Other days, it's simply getting out of bed, taking a deep breath, and making it through the day.

Both are wins.

We live in a world that glorifies speed—where success is often measured by how quickly we achieve milestones. But real progress isn't about speed. It's about consistency. It's about showing up, even when you're exhausted. It's about taking just one step forward, even when it feels like you're crawling.

Because stopping? That's not an option. **Forward is the only option.**

There will be times in life when you feel stuck, overwhelmed, or defeated. You might feel like you're not making enough progress, like the weight of everything you're carrying is too heavy. Every small step forward is still movement.

It doesn't matter how slow you go. It doesn't matter if today's progress looks tiny compared to yesterday's. What matters is that you don't stop. Once you stop, once you give in to the idea that it's too hard, too exhausting, too much—you risk staying stuck forever.

The key is to keep moving, no matter what that movement looks like.

Ask yourself: What is one small, manageable step I can take today?

GIVE YOURSELF PERMISSION TO STRUGGLE, BUT NOT TO QUIT

Let's be honest: there will be days when you don't feel like moving forward. Days when it feels like the weight of everything is too much. On those days, it's okay to struggle. It's okay to feel frustrated, tired, or discouraged.

What's not okay is giving up entirely.

In Your Personal Life: If you're going through grief, trauma, or burnout, allow yourself to feel the emotions. Take time to rest. But don't mistake rest for stopping altogether. Even the smallest act—reaching out for support, journaling your thoughts, or simply breathing through the hard moments—is a step forward.

In Your Professional Life: If you face failure, rejection, or setbacks, resist the urge to see them as signs to quit. Every successful person has faced obstacles. The difference between those who succeed and those who don't is simple: the ones who succeed keep going.

Ask yourself: Am I allowing myself space to rest and struggle while still committing to moving forward?

ACKNOWLEDGE THAT YOUR SURVIVAL IS PROOF OF YOUR STRENGTH

When life has dragged you through the fire, it's easy to focus on what's been burned—the broken dreams, the relationships that didn't last, the moments when you thought, *This might be the thing that finally breaks me.* And even when you manage to keep going, it's not uncommon to carry the weight of shame, regret, or self-doubt, convinced that your scars are signs of weakness.

Those scars aren't signs of damage—they're symbols of strength. They mean you made it through. You didn't just survive—you endured. You didn't just keep breathing—you kept becoming. That matters more than any applause or validation ever could.

Strength isn't found in those who've had it easy. It's found in those who've been cracked open by life, who've crawled out of their darkest chapters and still chose to stand back up—again and again. I've spent years looking at my own story, wondering if it made me too much or not enough. Every time I revisit the pain I've walked through, I'm reminded: I didn't just walk through hell—I rebuilt my life in the ashes. So did you. You might not even realize how powerful that is. You've normalized survival to the point where you've forgotten—it's something not everyone could have done. YOU did.

So no, you're not weak because you still cry. You're not broken because it still hurts. You're not behind because your healing took longer than someone else's. You are strong because you're still here. You're still standing. You're still willing to grow. Let your survival be your proof—not that you were perfect, but that you were **unstoppable.**

In Your Personal Life: Instead of dwelling on what almost broke you, start recognizing the resilience it built in you. You are stronger than you give yourself credit for, and you have the power to use your experiences as fuel—not chains.

In Your Professional Life: Your past struggles have given you skills that make you a stronger leader, a more empathetic team member, and a more determined professional. Recognize that your ability to overcome obstacles is a strength, not a weakness.

Ask yourself: What have I survived that has made me stronger? How can I use that strength to push forward?

YOUR LIFE HAS MEANING

Even When You Can't See It

There will be days when you question why you're here. When the weight of your struggles feels unbearable. When you wonder if any of it matters.

Here's the truth: If you were not meant to be here, you wouldn't be.

You have survived every difficult moment, every painful chapter, every dark season—not by accident, but because your story isn't finished. You are here because there is still something you are meant to do. There are people you are meant to help, lessons you are meant to teach, and moments you are meant to experience that will change everything.

It's not about waiting for a grand revelation of purpose. Your purpose is unfolding every single day in the way you show up, the way you fight through, and the way you refuse to quit.

- You have survived for a reason.
- You are still here because your story isn't finished.
- Your existence is not an accident—your life has meaning.

No matter what you've been through, no matter how broken or exhausted you may feel at times, you are not here just to exist. You are here to live, to grow, to impact, to thrive. Don't waste another second doubting your worth. Don't let the past convince you that your future isn't bright. Don't let the hardships you've faced make you forget that you were meant for more. You are here. That means you have a purpose.

Pain is something we all face—none of us are immune to it. It is a universal part of the human experience. What truly sets people apart is what they choose to do with their pain. You can let it consume you, become the loudest voice in your story, or you can choose to turn it into something greater. **Pain without purpose is just suffering—but pain given purpose becomes power.**

I've chosen to take the deepest wounds in my life and turn them into light for others. I've taken what was meant to break me and turned it into a foundation to build something stronger. My past may have shaped parts of me, but it does not own me. I am no longer living just to survive—I'm living to thrive. And if you're reading this, I need you to know: *You can, too.*

You are not defined by the pain you've endured. You are defined by the strength it revealed. I've been through trauma, loss, exhaustion, and chaos. Life has tried again and again to take me out. I refuse to let any of it tell me who I am. I am not just a survivor—I am a fighter. A builder. A leader. A woman who refuses to be counted out.

And you? You are more powerful than you know. You're still standing. Still rising. Still finding your way through. The fire may have come for you, but it did not win. We are not here by accident. **The fire was meant to destroy us—but we? We rise from it.**

Suzanne Saunders-O'Herron is a leadership and talent development specialist who focuses on helping organizations create well-rounded leaders who are targeted towards creating whole-person workplaces that balance productivity and performance with their people operations.

Suzanne has two master's degrees in education and is near completion of her doctorate in leadership studies. In addition to her degrees, Suzanne has multiple certifications in a variety of fields, including being certified as a Neurolinguistic Programmer, John Reid® Investigator, Interviewer & Persuader, AI Content Generator, Personality Assessment Evaluator, Project Manager, and more.

Suzanne is a published author and grant writer and has founded multiple nonprofit organizations. She has a vast career history working in the tool & die industry, healthcare and developmental disability fields, and manufacturing and retail industries, as well as in education.

She offers services through her consulting company for talent development, process improvement and strategic marketing, in addition to her project management, talent and leadership development, branded event planning, and human resources services.

Suzanne is an advocate for mental health services for all in need, particularly children, veterans, and employees, and acts as a parent advocate with a local mental health agency. She has co-hosted a Mental Health Gala and is working to establish her own mental health and life transformation agency. She is assisting her husband in their creation of the "Mag Dump Your Demons (™)" brand focused on a call to action for veterans with mental health needs.

Suzanne has a blended family with her military-veteran husband, which includes her two stepdaughters, two adopted children, and their biological son. They live on a farm in Northwest, Ohio, with their horses, cats, goats, dogs, and a pig named Barbie-Q.

To connect with Suzanne:

Personally: @OurWackadoodleLife

—

Professionally: https://www.facebook.com/profile.php?id=61580114115925

www.ingramcontent.com/pod-product-compliance
Lightning Source LLC
LaVergne TN
LVHW020928090426
835512LV00020B/3259